TO THE NEXT STEP

TO THE NEXT STEP

YOUR GUIDE FROM HIGH SCHOOL
AND COLLEGE TO THE REAL WORLD

BY KYLE GRAPPONE

atmosphere press

To My Wife, Kayla

Thank you for your support and for always keeping me calm. Everything I do is for you and our family.

To My Parents

Thank you for understanding that I want more out of life and supporting all of my projects without question. I'm lucky to have people like you who believe in me.

To Eric

I hope I make you proud. Miss you and love you every day.

CONTENTS

Chapter 1:
The Part of Life
You Don't See Coming

"Well, that's just life." I like to believe that this was the moment where my life changed. It wasn't an earth-shattering revelation, but rather the day the wheels in my head started turning. It was a Sunday afternoon in 2013. I point out the year to demonstrate this was a little over 3 years since I graduated college. It was a Sunday, and I had just arrived back home from a trip. At the time, I lived with my parents and was speaking with my mom. I was complaining about having to go to work the next day. Most Americans have a similar complaint, so my mother didn't have any sympathy for me. I explained that my job was boring, unfulfilling, and a waste of my time. I continued to explain that my life had become a dull cycle of going to work and coming home and that I missed the days of doing the things that I enjoyed doing. This is when she dropped that line on me, that this was just the way life was supposed to be. She then left the room.

As I mentioned, it is not as if my life changed forever that day. The real world does not work like that. However, 5 years later, I still have not forgotten about it. In the coming years, I worked a few different marketing jobs. At the time, they all seemed to be different, but looking back on it now, they were all the same. They were in different positions with different responsibilities in various industries, but for me, they were all the same because they were all unfulfilling. We will reference my personal journey throughout this book. For now, let's talk about how this relates to you.

As I worked my way through the "corporate world," I began to notice a disturbing trend. The majority of the people I worked with seemed to dislike their jobs. I'm not talking about being occasionally stressed or tired. I am talking about a persistent feeling of anger, resentment, and depression. My coworkers were always complaining about something. Whether it was waiting for 5 pm, wishing for the weekend, or the fact that it was Monday, they seemingly hated being at their jobs, and worse, were dissatisfied with the type of person they had become. The other trend that was growing apparent was that this notion was universally accepted as fact. Hence, my mother's comment about the way life is supposed to be.

In 2013, Gallup released a poll that stated that 70% of Americans were disengaged from their jobs.

I began looking into this. Was I crazy? Was I working with the wrong people? Is it possible that the majority of workers in this country feel this way? That was a pretty big claim, and I needed to see if I was onto something. As I spoke to more people, created surveys, and had open conversations, I began to confirm that this notion was correct. People tend to dislike their jobs and are unhappy with parts or all of the life they are living. It wasn't just the people I was speaking to, either. In 2013, Gallup released a poll that stated that 70% of Americans were disengaged from their jobs. That is a staggering number. Your job is where you spend the majority of your time and energy. If you are unhappy there, how can you expect to build a happy life overall?

Once I determined there was an issue worth exploring, I had to figure out why. Why is this happening, and what, if anything, can we do to stop it? I began to send out surveys to people I knew, asking them questions about their education and job satisfaction. I also started to openly discuss this with contacts of different ages, races, genders, and backgrounds. What I discovered is the basis for this entire book. There are several possible reasons that someone is unhappy with his or her job. A primary reason people become this way is that there is a part of life that, as students, they never see coming. College, and ultimately the real world, carries with it several elements that students have no idea they need to prepare for. And when they don't prepare, they end up drowning in a sea of confusion and chaos. Surrounded by those who convince them that this is the only way to live their life. I wrote this book to tell you: there is another way.

We are taught from a very young age to learn as much as you can, work hard, and achieve a well-paying job.

Before we get to that, allow me to expand on this part of life I just mentioned. This part of life that I will be mentioning quite often in this conversation. Society often makes mention of "the real world," sometimes calling it the corporate or working world. It refers to being an adult—and everything that comes along with it, such as working full time, taking care of yourself, starting a family, and a ton of other things that consume your day-to-day life. From a young age, we know that it is there. As we go to school, we know that we are being educated to prepare for this world. We are taught from a young age to learn as much as you can, work hard, and achieve a high-paying job. That's all well and good, but everything I just said is pretty broad. It lacks details, specifics, and examples. It also tends to lead us down one path and has us focusing very much on the present, and very little on the future.

Combine these two stats, and your day job has now consumed 65%, or nearly two-thirds, of your life.

It's important to identify what being an adult and working full time actually entails. To explain what I mean, I will use numbers. A 7-day week has in it, 168 hours. Let's say you sleep 7 hours a night. Now, this may seem like a lot for a current student; however, you have to understand that as you get older, you need more sleep than you are getting now. Plus, you are going to be more tired because you are working longer hours. So, when we subtract those 49 hours from our total, we arrive at 119 hours. When you work full time, you work a minimum of 35–40 hours. Add on 2 hours a day to account for getting ready in the morning, commuting, traffic, and overtime, and we arrive at roughly 50 hours, or 30%, of your week. Combine these two stats, and your day job has now consumed 65%, or nearly two-thirds, of your life. You also have to add in the time and energy it takes to complete adult tasks such as cooking, cleaning, laundry, and grocery shopping. The wide-open, responsibility-free schedule you enjoy now changes rapidly. If you are not enjoying some aspect of your chosen profession, then you will spend the majority of your time, and ultimately life, unhappy.

Now, I am not saying you are doomed for a life of misery or that the best parts of your life are happening now, and you have no hope of topping them when you become an adult. On the contrary, I am beginning to paint the picture of what awaits you years from now. The reason people feel this way is not because this type of life is inevitable, but rather because they were unprepared and did not know it was coming. That is the whole point of my book and my message. Cheer up! You're going to be okay.

If you are not enjoying some aspect of your chosen profession, then you will spend the majority of your time, and ultimately life, unhappy.

The real world brings with it challenges that young people cannot even think of yet. Let's continue talking about your job. We have discussed how much of your time it takes up. It's also worth noting that unlike your past part-time jobs, you need this one for survival. Life is expensive. You may have heard your parents say this before. It's true. The older you get, the more things you have to pay for, and the only way you can pay for those things is with the salary from your job. You need some occupation, producing an income, to merely provide enough money to live your day-to-day life. If you are unhappy or want to do something else, that's okay, but it's not like you can quit your job and pursue what will make you happy. There are rules now.

NOTE: as you go through the real world, you will learn about other ways to earn income, such as owning a business, investing in real estate, and the like. A typical 9-to-5 job is not the only way to earn money. However, for the sake of our conversation, we are going to focus on that type of work because it is what you are going to be entering into right out of college.

If you have graduated from college, you most likely have student loans. Again, let's use numbers to break this down. The average American college costs about $33,480 a year, or $133,920 in total, assuming you graduate in 4 years. If you take out loans to cover that entire cost, you are paying an additional $49,706 in interest alone. Your new total is $183,626. If you agree to pay this back over 15 years, you will be paying about $1,020 per month. This is, by far, the most significant expense you have ever had in your life up to this point. You are required by law to pay this back. Your paycheck just went from a nice-to-have bonus to a need-to-have requirement in the blink of an eye.

It is worth mentioning that most students do not take out that much in loans. We are going to talk about that process in detail later on, but that monthly amount could be a lot less. The point is, if you need loans to cover college, you will have an additional monthly expense that you are not used to. This monthly payment will most likely force you to keep a job, even if you do not like it.

Let's bring back in those pesky real-world things we talked

about earlier. An entry-level salary in the state of New Jersey is $45,570. I would urge you to research this information for your state. My entry-level salary was $35,000. Again, we will get to why that was in a little bit. After taxes, you are taking home $2,900 per month. Again, do your research regarding your state taxes. This may be the most money you have ever made in your life. However, do not forget the student loans we just spoke about. After you deduct that monthly payment, you are left with a little less than $1,900. Are you planning on moving out of your parents' house after college? Average rent in New Jersey is about $1,400 a month. You are now left with $400 to spend on bills and groceries. I am giving you New Jersey numbers because that is where I live, and I encourage each of you to take the time to research your state and not go off national numbers. Do not rely on anyone to provide you with the information that you are more than capable of finding on your own.

Once you accept a position and start making life choices on the basis of your salary, it becomes increasingly difficult to make substantial shifts such as a new career, launching a new business, or taking extended time off.

Now, these numbers will differ and might not be so high. The point I am trying to make is that the job you have plays a significant part in your life. Once you accept a position and start making life choices on the basis of your salary, it becomes increasingly difficult to make substantial shifts, such as a new career, launching a new business, or taking extended time off.

It is not impossible, but if you wait until you are in your mid-20s to care about your career, you will have many more obstacles than if you started planning when you were in high school or college.

Being responsible for yourself and your well-being is challenging enough. However, as you get older, you may become responsible for the well-being of other people, such as your spouse and kids. I understand if things like marriage and family are miles away from your thoughts as a student, but just be prepared that the day will arrive when other human beings will rely on you for things. It will be your job to provide for them, and you owe it to all of you to be as prepared as possible for when that day arrives.

Outside of finances and responsibility, it's crucial to understand how the corporate world operates. The primary purpose of almost every single business is to make money. Even nonprofits are working to fund a mission and pay their bills. Companies are built to produce profits and make someone money on a daily basis. This is something people take very seriously, and they are only going to hire you if you can make them money. The hard truth is that they do not care about your student loans, your high school achievements, or that your parents think you are a great person. They care about the value you can provide. If you cannot make them money, or worse, are costing them money, they will remove you from the equation. That's the harsh reality of corporate America.

Again, I do not say this to deter you but rather to prepare you. You can end up working with awesome people at amazing companies that do great work. You need to understand what is going to be expected of you. Furthermore, once you start a career path in a specific line of work, it becomes difficult to switch to something new. Companies, driven by profits, want to spend money on employees who have the highest probability of returning the desired result. Therefore, they are more likely to hire someone who has direct experience in that field. If you wait too long to find your passions, you will lack the expertise necessary to switch into the role you want. You may also be unable to take a lesser role because it will be less money and you cannot afford it because of the obligations we just spoke about.

This is not the entire picture of what growing up looks like. You will experience beautiful moments like getting your first place, marriage, family, promotions, and so much more. These are all parts of life that you are aware of. What we are doing here is talking about the part of life that TV shows don't cover. Bill Gates once said, "TV is not your life. In real life, people have to leave the coffee shop to go to their jobs." Life, while it can be wonderful, can also be hard and challenging. This is precisely the part of life that most students don't see coming.

If you don't know something is about to happen, how can you prepare for it? The answer is you cannot. So, you get stuck thinking about what's right in front of you. The math test next week, what your weekend plans are with your friends, and the latest problem in your life, which, when compared with adult problems, really isn't much of a problem at all. This is the mistake that so many of those who have come before you, including me, have made. This is how we have arrived at our current state of dissatisfaction.

In this book, we are going to cover high school, selecting a college, your college experience, graduating, and the real world that awaits you. This book was written by a college graduate who has interviewed, surveyed, and researched countless of other high school and college graduates. The mission of this book is to prepare you for life's challenges and to prevent you from ending up blindsided by the real world. Do I have your attention now? Good. Let's move forward.

CHAPTER 2:
WHY SHOULD YOU CARE?

Everyone has something to say, and thanks to social media, everyone has a platform to say it. Just because someone has something to say doesn't mean it's valuable, and it definitely does not mean you should care. Your time is valuable, and if you are going to dedicate the next few hours to reading this book, I owe you an explanation as to why you should care about what I have to say, and more importantly, how this directly affects you, your life, and your future.

We have become a society that has made being miserable for 8 hours a day into rational behavior.

Like I mentioned earlier, I started this journey based on two things I noticed while working in the real world. First, the never-ending trend of people who dislike their jobs and are dissatisfied with the type of life they are living. Second, the widely accepted notion that you are supposed to hate your job and that there is nothing you can do about it. Those two revelations are what started this mission. This idea that so many people were unhappy was something that I could not just accept as fact. We have become a society that has made being miserable for 8 hours a day into rational behavior. Not only did I have to figure out how this happened but I also felt the need to prevent this from happening to anyone else.

With all that being said, what has kept it going is everything I have learned in my research along the way. When I started writing blog posts, delivering keynote speeches, and writing this book I knew that I wanted my content to be more than just my thoughts. It has always been important to me that my advice is backed up by data and similar information from other people. If I were the only one who felt this way, then it would just be one person ranting. That is hardly an excuse for anyone to spend time and money on a book.

Furthermore, if I was going to make this claim—that there is a large number of people who are unprepared for the next steps in their lives—then I have to find a way to back that up. Stats are fine, and some will be presented later on, but I wanted to showcase real situations, real human stories that show what happens when you don't care about your future. I wanted this book to be an instruction manual for students, but also an outlet for adults to dispense real-world wisdom in an attempt to inspire those students to think differently about how they approach their educations, futures, and lives overall.

The issues and solutions presented in this book are a result of speaking to high school and college graduates of various ages about what their life has been like out in the real world. It's about what they did in high school, how they handled their time in college, and their honest first experiences in the real world. It's a story of what happens to you when you don't take advantage of the opportunities in front of you. It's also a story of what happens when you do.

WHY SHOULD YOU CARE?

Your life changes forever after you graduate college.

I understand that if you are between the ages of 14–21, it may be difficult to grasp what the next 60–70 years of your life will be like. It's a lot easier to understand what I am talking about at my age (30) because of how much I have seen since graduation. You tend to experience and learn more about life after just a few short years in the real world than you do while you are in school. Life comes at you pretty fast after graduation. Here's what I mean:

Your life changes forever after you graduate college. You are no longer a student. That fact doesn't just apply to the classroom. Up until now being a student may have meant that your parents did a lot of things for you. This includes paying for the roof over your head, cooking your meals, paying bills, going grocery shopping, and making your doctors' appointments for you. Becoming an adult and entering the real world means taking care of yourself. All those things that I just mentioned take time and money.

Not being a student anymore means that learning is no longer your only responsibility. There is a lot that will be expected of you. You are not a child anymore, and I don't think students, me included, really understood what that meant until it was too late. To understand what that means as a student, I want you to make a list of every single thing your parents currently do for you and every single bill or expense they cover. Then, try your best to assign a number of hours that each task takes. Then attach a cost to each expense. It should look something like this:

Tasks

Grocery Shopping: 1–2 hours per week

Cooking: 10 hours per week

Cleaning: 1 hour per week

Laundry: 3 hours per week

Expenses

Rent/Utilities: $2,000 per month

Groceries/Household Needs: $400 per month

Cell Phone: $100 per month

Cable/Internet: $100 per month

Auto Insurance: $100 per month

These numbers are a rough estimate, but it makes the point. You are taking on a lot when you become an adult. You will have less time and money. I don't say this to scare you—I say it to prepare you. Having less time means you need to enjoy what you do for a living on some level. Otherwise, you will end up miserable, unfulfilled, and wishing your life away because you ended up in a situation you didn't plan for. These expenses point out the importance of having a well-paying job. The importance of developing a skill set that will consistently create opportunities. It also demonstrates how difficult it is to start over or to take a lower-paying job.

Another primary expectation is that you are going to find a job and contribute to society. The way you view work will have to change. Up to this point, you may have only worked part time. This leaves plenty of hours for fun stuff, and most of the money you made probably went toward that fun stuff. Working full time is a whole different situation. Allow me to use some numbers from Chapter 1 to break this down again for you:

- Number of Hours in a Week: 168
- Number of Hours for Sleep: 49 (7 per night, 7 nights a week)
- Number of "Awake Hours": 119
- Full-Time Job: 50 (see below)
- Number of Hours Taken Up: 99 out of 168 (about 60% of your week)

It's also important to understand the role money plays in your life. You will hear a lot of people say that money doesn't buy happiness. While this is true, lack of money can certainly bring stress and pain. Like it or not, the world we all live in runs on money. The things you need to live and the things you want to have all cost money. Much of the stuff we need and want in life has a cost attached to it. I am talking about things such as a nice place to live (rent/mortgage), a good car to drive (gas, car insurance), a way to keep up with friends (cell phone/smartphone), entertainment (internet, cable), feeling well and healthy (gym membership, health insurance), and a solid education (student loans). More importantly, all these costs have a company behind them, expecting to be paid on a weekly or monthly basis. That company does not care about your feelings or your life situation. Bills need to be paid, regardless of what might be going on in your life at the time. This is why your career is so crucial. You need to be prepared to build a career that will allow you to earn enough over your lifetime to pay all these expenses and have enough left over to enjoy your life outside of work.

The expenses that were once covered by your parents will now be up to you to pay. A lot changes very quickly, and if you are not prepared from Day 1, it can have a serious impact on your life. All of these expenses take money out of your paycheck. If you end up with a job that doesn't pay well, because you didn't put in the effort or weren't prepared, then how can you expect to do anything fun after you've paid all your bills? As I said, the companies on the other end of those bills are waiting to be paid. This is one of the reasons that so many people are living lives of dissatisfaction. They were not prepared for this part of life and they are now struggling to get by in jobs they do not like.

Speaking of bills, if you took out student loans, you will soon, after graduation, be expected to pay those back. As we covered in Chapter 1, they will cost a significant amount of money for a long time, so how much you earn is going to be an essential part of any career decision you make. If you take out what is called a federal loan, you are put on a schedule to pay that back over 10 years. However, as studies have shown, students who earn a bachelor's degree are taking closer to 20 years to pay it back. So, whatever amount you take out, you need to understand that you will be repaying that loan for many years to come. You will need to select a career path that pays enough to do this and, ideally, is something that you will find some sort of satisfaction in doing for an extended period of time. When I speak about aspects of the real world that students do not know are coming, this is exactly what I mean.

Put it another way: if you float your way through high school and college, doing just enough to get by and refusing to plan for your future, you will probably have to take whatever job comes to you. You will be forced to take this desperation job because you have to pay back your student loans. So, while you may be gaining experience, you are doing it in an industry that does not interest you. Once you realize that you are in the wrong line of work, you may decide to change course. Here is the problem, though. Companies value experience. The positions you may now want will require expertise that you don't have. The jobs that will be open to you won't pay as well, because they will be more entry level because you lack the experience needed. Chances are, if you have student loans and adult bills, you might not be able to afford to start over. Maybe you will, but isn't it worth trying your best to get it right the first time? At the very least, you can identify where you want to end up in your life, so that if you do have to change careers, you'll be better prepared. If you are unable to make the career change you desire, you may end up getting stuck in an industry that you don't like because you lack the experience to get paid enough in something else.

If you are removing things from your life that bring you joy, shouldn't you make sure that what you are replacing them with something brings you some pleasure as well?

I point all of this out because life is different after graduation. The differences are the things that students do not see coming. You have a lot less free time. You have to wake up every day at a particular time. Depending on your job, you may need to be in one place for 8 hours every day. That's a long time to do something you don't like. You are also only allowed a certain amount of days off. You will not be able to pick and choose what you get to do with your friends. You won't always get to go do something fun like go to the beach or a baseball game.

If you are removing things from your life that bring you joy, shouldn't you make sure that what you are replacing them with brings you some pleasure as well? If you have to get up early every day, wear nice clothes, and work hard, shouldn't you be doing something that makes an impact? Wouldn't it be nice to do something that fulfills and satisfies you on some level?

God willing, you will be an adult for a long time. You will live in this real world for decades. You owe it to yourself to set yourself up for a life of happiness and fulfillment. Too many people have taken an "I'll figure it out later" mentality and then been stuck in a career that brings them nothing but stress and disappointment. Everything I mentioned above contributes to why people are so dissatisfied with their lives. For example, when I started my research, I created a survey to send to college graduates. One of the survey questions asked what was something they felt unprepared for after graduation. The majority of the recent grads listed finances and budgeting as their answer. Most went on to say that they had no idea how to handle their finances and desperately wished that someone had told them how to do this.

Another question I asked was regarding what a public speaker should tell high school and college students in a speech. The respondents were very detailed and passionate in their responses. You could honestly tell that they had things they needed to get off their chest and advice they desperately wanted to dispense. One of the most common answers centered around the importance of "starting now" when talking about topics such as planning for your future, making contacts, and focusing on your schoolwork. Another common answer was the importance of learning and exploring your options. Too many people hold themselves to pursuing one type of job and never stop to consider the alternatives that are open to them.

The last question I asked them was what they would do differently if given the opportunity to go back to school and do it all over again. The answers were wide ranging, but the common theme was that they would have done *more*. Some would have studied more. Others would have better explored their options regarding majors or classes they could have taken. The point is that these people did not do all they could. They were left with some level of regret regarding how their life had turned out so far. This does not mean that they were all wholly miserable or did not enjoy their life at some points. It merely says that they wished they could go back and do more to create an even better life. This is what happens when you are not adequately prepared for the next steps in your life.

I want you to imagine yourself standing on a road, about to start a journey. This journey is called "the rest of your life." At several points, you will come to a fork in the road, a point in the journey where you have to choose which path to take. One way will be easy and not require a significant amount effort. You won't have to do a lot of work if you choose this option. The other path you could take is more difficult. It's challenging and confusing. If those are the only facts presented to you, it's pretty clear which one you would take. Most people would choose the easy path because all they know is how things will be in the short term. What they don't know is where these paths lead. The easy way may seem tempting, but it often does not lead to the life you want. The hard path may look intimidating, but you will end up in a much better place. This is the dilemma that so many have faced, and most have made the wrong choice. They took the easy path and are now stuck in a destination they never intended to be.

If someone came back in time from the future, and told you what your particular future was going to be like, you would listen to that person, right? This book is as close as it's going to get to that scenario. This is a manual that is going to break down the next steps in your life. The graduates I have spoken to and I are currently living the part of life that you will someday enter. Basically, we are from your future—and we're here to tell you what's coming next.

CHAPTER 3:

WHAT TYPE OF PERSON DO YOU WANT TO BECOME?

The goal of most Americans is to retire at or around the age of 65. This is something we are made aware of our entire lives. When we are children, we notice that our grandparents are not working because they have retired. When you are older, your parents eventually reach this age and retire themselves. When you enter the workforce, money gets deducted for social security, and you will pay into something called a 401(k). You know that retirement is coming at some point in your life; therefore, you prepare for it. You begin saving money at a young age and ideally save more as time goes on. The bottom line—you know it's on the way, so you prepare accordingly.

The idea of working a full-time job is not that different. Working full time is not a new concept that has appeared in the last 10 years. It has been happening for generations. Your parents worked full time, as did their parents, and their parents' parents. How is it that so many people are so unprepared for something that they have spent their entire lives being told is on its way?

Have you ever been asked the question "What do you want to be when you grow up?"? Chances are you have. You have probably been asked this question several times throughout your life. Therein lies the problem. This is a fundamentally flawed question. It's flawed because it is asking you to choose without having all the facts. It's a question that can significantly affect the rest of your life, and you are being forced to answer it without understanding all your choices. It is just unfair to ask someone at the age of 10, 15, or even 18 years old to decide what career they want to have for the *rest of their lives*. But we do it anyway.

We ask elementary school students to write essays based on this answer. We ask middle school kids to create presentations based on this answer. Then, worst of all, we ask high school students to choose a college based on this answer. We are literally asking students to make a life-altering choice without a full understanding of their options. So, you take a guess. You choose something that sounds like it could be cool. You pick a career that the internet tells you will make you a ton of money, or you select something based on what your parents tell you to do.

If you decide that the career you want to pursue is outside the norm, be prepared for there to be concern on your parents' side.

While we are here, let's talk about your parents and their role in the choices that shape your future. The number one job of any parent is to keep you safe. It is not to make you happy. They may want you to be happy, but that is not their primary goal. If they have to choose between your well-being and your happiness, they will always choose what they think is going to keep you safe. I mention this because they might not always support your choices in the way that you want. It does not mean that they do not want you to be happy. If they feel the choices you are making regarding your college selection, career, and future are potentially going to hurt or disappoint you in any way, their likely reaction will be to steer you back to a safe choice. If you decide that the career you want to pursue is outside the norm, be prepared for there to be concern on your parents' side.

For example, let's say you want to be an actor. It is incredibly difficult to make a living as an actor, and the hard truth is that most people who try do not become one. If you make it known to your parents that this is your goal, their natural reaction will be fear of your failing. This is not because they do not believe in you. It is because they know that the odds, no matter how hard you try, are against you. They know that if you fail, you will be hurt, and your pain causes them pain. They are also going to naturally think about what you will do after it does not work out. They feel this way because they know how the real world is and the importance of having a backup plan.

If you genuinely want to be an actor, singer, author, or any other type of uncommon job, you need to understand what lies ahead. It will be difficult; it always is when you try to beat the odds. Furthermore, you may need to take a job you don't like while you pursue this dream. It's vital you understand that this will be something that takes time and that you do not give up just because it takes longer than you expected. Do what you need to do to support yourself, but never give up working toward that goal. Remember, you are the only one that has to live your life day in and day out. You owe it to yourself to chase whatever dream you want.

It's normal for your parents to feel this way; this does not mean you should not pursue your dream job. This admonition does not mean you should select a career that makes your parents happy. It merely says you need to understand that you are an adult now, your choices are your own, and you need to take ownership of your life choices and goals. If you are prepared and feel confident in your choice, then you owe it yourself to pursue it. Your parents will come around, I promise.

Another item worth pointing out regarding your parents and older generations is this: the generations that grew up before us lived in very different times. There was no internet or social media. You did not work from home. Most companies did things manually instead of the automated processes that have been put in place.

Most importantly, there was a lot more company loyalty 20 years ago. Decades ago, it was common to stay at a job for a long time or even your entire career. This was because companies were able to be loyal to their employees, and the employees, in turn, felt comfortable committing to one company and not looking for other positions. Times have changed. Technological advances have forced companies to rethink their workforce constantly. Loyalty to profits has replaced loyalty to employees. Employees feel much less inclined to stay loyal to a company that could lay them off at any time, regardless of performance. This is why you need to do your research and make your own informed choices, decide what is best for you and your life. You need to own your future.

Back to that terrible question that forces you to decide your career before you even understand what working full time entails: What do you want to be when you grow up? This question is the root of our problem. It is a primary reason that so many generations, despite years of warnings, are unprepared for what awaits them in life. Therefore, we need to agree to change this question. More importantly, you, as a student, need to stop asking yourself this question, and if you are reading this as a parent or educator, you should stop asking this of your kids and students. Instead, begin to ask them this: *What type of person do you want to become?*

When we ask that question, the entire narrative changes. You are no longer handcuffed to one job or one career, but rather to an idea of the type of person you want to be and the type of impact you want to have on the world around you. To find the answer to this question, you need to draw from your life and past experiences. What have you done that has brought you the most joy and fulfillment? When it comes to interacting with other people, what makes you happy and feel good? Think about your past but also apply it to your future actions. Be aware of what you are doing that brings you the most fulfillment and makes you feel complete.

For example, let's say you are the type of person who other people go to for advice. You enjoy listening to and solving their problems. It brings you joy when you see someone is happier, calmer, and more confident after talking to you. That means you might want to become the type of person who helps people in need of help. This could mean becoming a psychologist. However, if you enjoy working with kids, it could mean being a guidance counselor or teacher.

You are no longer handcuffed to one job or one career, but rather to an idea of the type of person you want to be and the type of impact you want to have on the world around you.

Another example, one that I can relate to, is the need to entertain people. I enjoy making people laugh and ultimately making them happy. I also know I am the type of person who needs to be always moving around and doing things. This tells me two things. First, my career should be focused on creating something that other people will enjoy. It could entertain, help, or educate them, but I should be the one creating it. The second is that I should focus my studies toward jobs and careers that do not center on sitting at the same office desk every day.

I could give you so many more examples, but hopefully, you get the point. Begin thinking about what type of person you want to become, and that could help lead to what you'd consider doing for the 30-40 years you anticipate working after college. When you retire, what type of person do you want to tell people you *were*? Do you want to be able to talk about a career in which you helped hundreds of people lead better lives, or helped thousands become smarter, or just helped people feel a little happier? Asking this type of question can help you start to build the future you will want to live in.

However, if you are working toward something you care about, then you are growing into the best possible version of yourself, and you will be able to create a career that leaves you fulfilled on a regular basis.

Once you determine the answer(s), you can start building the life you want. You can begin building a life that will bring you joy and fulfillment. Notice how I do not mention happiness. Happiness is different. Many things in life can make you happy, but this doesn't mean they should be your job or career. I also want to point out that regardless of what you choose to do, it will still be difficult at times. You will have stressful days. There will always be days where it will feel like work, and it will be hard to find that joy and fulfillment. You will also still look forward to the weekend because it means spending time with your family and friends. However, if you are working toward something you care about, then you are growing into the best possible version of yourself, and you will be able to create a career that leaves you fulfilled on a regular basis.

We will start by figuring out what type of person you want to become and how that relates to finding the right job and career for you. Like we said before, it's important to figure out what in your day-to-day life brings you joy and fulfillment. What do you do for other people that makes you feel satisfied after you do it? For example, let's say you enjoy entertaining people. You feel at your best when you are making people laugh and causing them to have a good time. Perhaps, you should become the type of person who, in some way, entertains other people for a living. Now, the most obvious answer might be to become an actor. While there is nothing wrong with that, it's crucial to think much broader. We need to think about all the types of career paths associated with the idea of entertaining. This could include roles in front of a camera, such as an actor, news anchor, or comedian. It could also include various positions behind the camera, such as a scriptwriter or technician. It could also mean careers that have nothing to do with TV. Perhaps you should become a writer. Someone who writes articles or books that are continually entertaining people in some way. Maybe all you need to do is work for a company in the entertainment business. This could include working for a company as a marketer or event planner. The possibilities are endless, but as long as you know you are working toward a life filled with making people happy, you will know you are living the life you were meant to live.

We are going to cover in the coming chapter how to identify the different types of roles in various industries that may align with your idea of the type of person you want to become. For now, you just need to start answering those questions and figuring out what your interests and passions could be.

You have to get up every day and live this life; you owe it to yourself to build an experience that you want to live.

Let's go back a second and talk about being an actor. We are going to use acting as an example, but this will serve as a stand-in for any other outside-the-box career, such as singer, social media influencer, or anything else that seems like a stretch. If you truly believe you want to pursue a job that is not of the everyday variety, you should not let anything stop you. As I mentioned before, your family may not be as supportive. They don't want to see you get hurt. But you need to push forward, because you are the only one living your life. You have to get up every day and live this life; you owe it to yourself to build an experience that you want to live.

Here is something else that is extremely important. If you dare to chase a dream, some people will get very upset with you. They won't come out and admit it. They will mask it with something else like "caring for you," but they will be upset. They will be upset because you have awoken something in them that they tried to push down inside themselves. You have reminded them that they never pursued their dreams. You need to tune these people out and stay focused on the life you want to live.

Yes, pursuing a career that most do not have makes it much more challenging. The critical thing to realize is that just because it does not happen immediately does not mean the dream is over forever. Too many people give up after one setback and end up living a mediocre life instead of the exceptional one they dreamed of. If you are chasing a unique career, you need to put a plan in place. What do you need to get there? Yes, this includes high school and college, but it also includes your life after college. It is entirely possible that you may not achieve this dream job right after college. Understand that you may need to take a regular office job to pay your bills. You may need to do this for a few years. Remember, your life is long, and so is your career. It is worth making that sacrifice now to achieve the life you want down the road. If you are lucky enough to identify exactly what you want in life, do not let any person or situation take that away from you.

Hopefully now you are starting to think about the type of person you want to become. Don't worry—you don't have to figure this out overnight. However, you should start building this person in your head sooner rather than later so all those important decisions can be made with this type of person in mind. But that is only half the battle. The reason we want to become this person is so we can build a life we will be happy to live. We want to determine what type of life we want, and then we need to figure out how to get there.

I'd also like to point out something significant. No job, career, or life will be perfect and easy 100% of the time. That simply does not exist. Growing up and being an adult can be difficult. It will have challenges and hardships. It's important to understand that enjoying your career does not result in the absence of stress. Life can be very challenging and unpredictable. You will not enjoy every single day of your job. There is a very famous motivational quote that says, "Find a job that you love, and you will never work a day in your life." That's nonsense. Anything worth having in life involves hard work. Writing this book has brought me a lot of joy and fulfillment, but I have had to work hard. I have had to make sacrifices. Some people get married and stay together for over 40 years and live happy lives, but if you ask any one of them whether it has been hard at some point, they will all say yes. They will all describe the amount of hard work that goes into a marriage, a home, and a family. They will tell you it was hard, stressful, joyful, and worth it.

Finding a job or career that you love does not mean the there won't be stress or hard work. Finding a job you love means that the stress and hard work are worth it. It means that a sense of fulfillment and purpose also joins the stress and hard work. It's having a sense of knowing that what you are doing day in and day out is of your choosing. You know, every day, that you are living out the life you were meant to live and that someday you can look back on it and be proud.

WHAT TYPE OF PERSON DO YOU WANT TO BECOME?

Deciding what type of life you want means choosing what is important to you. It is perfectly okay to admit that you want a life filled with vacations, beach houses, and nice things. Placing importance on materialistic possessions does not make you a bad person. However, you need to understand that this will require a high salary and long hours of work away from your family. If you are okay with that, then you need to make the sacrifices necessary to make that happen.

For me, I want the type of life in which I can have the freedom to work where I want and when I want. It's important to me that I have an experience that allows me to enjoy the world around me and, most importantly, allows me to enjoy time with my children. I want to be there and enjoy the summer with them. I want to take them to school and see their baseball games. I don't want to miss out on their lives because I am stuck at a desk working an arbitrary amount of time, being forced to stay until 5 because of a "rule" that was created decades ago and very few companies have had the guts to change.

It may be difficult, but you should decide the type of life you want to live. If dressing up every day and sitting at a desk is what you want, that's okay. If you are someone who enjoys a routine and executing the tasks given to you by others, then that can be your goal. You can build a career you are proud of this way—don't let anyone, including me, make you feel otherwise.

However, if that type of life sounds less than ideal, then you need to start thinking about why exactly you feel this way. Society will try to mold you into the type of person who works 40 hours a week at a desk for the next 40 years of your life. It is up to you to build the life you want. Do you want the type of life that allows you to travel? Retire at 55? Would you rather work from home and focus on your projects instead of commuting to work and following a dress code? These are the things to be constantly thinking about.

This is also a decision that may lead you to realize that college might not be right for you. We will dive more deeply into that later on in Chapter 7, but this process will force you to think about the next steps in your educational process. If you want to be the type of person who builds things, works with their hands, and is continually moving around, it is a strong possibility that college is not the right choice for you. If you want the type of life that allows you to dress down, work hard, and not sit in one place for 8 hours, then college is most likely not for you. If you are starting to arrive at these answers, you need to explore alternative careers. Again, we will talk all about trade schools and these types careers in Chapter 7.

You are the only one who has to live your life. You have to be in it, every single day. Others may give advice and have an opinion, but they get to walk away from it, and they certainly do not have to live with the consequences. You have to live with your choices, and you owe it to yourself to explore these questions openly and honestly. Once you do, you can start taking action in your everyday life to build toward the person you want to be and the life you want to live.

Answering the questions I have posed in this chapter gives you a basis for all the choices about your future that you will need to make in high school and college. No longer will you have to make a decision and hope that it was the right one. Instead, you'll know you made the right call because you will know precisely why you made it. You will begin to make every decision with this person and this life in mind. Everything you do will build toward these things you are trying to accomplish.

In the upcoming chapters, we'll talk about specific choices you will have to make and how they can become easier and make more of an impact if you know what you are making those choices for. For now, take some time to think about what brings you joy in life. What do you think you want to do every day as a career? Start to build this life in your head as you read through the upcoming chapters.

Chapter 4:
Where Do I Start?

We have covered a lot of ground so far. We have discussed this massive part of life that you probably didn't understand. We challenged and then threw out an age-old question. We also started to think about what type of person we want to be for the rest of our lives. That is a lot to take in! If you feel overwhelmed, that's okay. We are going to talk through it all, step-by-step, in the coming chapters. I'm going to start at your freshman year of high school, cover your entire time there, then do a deep dive into the college selection process.

If you are reading this as a student who has already finished high school, these chapters are still very much worth reading, and I will explain why when we get there. Also, we will be exploring this widely accepted notion that you have to go to college. If you are currently a high school student who hates sitting in class all day, you will want to tune into that section! We will enter into college and walk through all types of situations and opportunities. However, before we get into all of that, we have to figure out how to start.

If you think you have time to do these things "down the road," I promise you, you do not.

So, as the chapter says, where do we start? As I've

mentioned, the journey you will be taking is a personal one. No one else can answer these questions or make these choices for you. This book is about taking ownership of your education, future, and life. If you think you have time to do these things "down the road," I promise you, you do not. If you want to live a life you enjoy, you need to take control of that life right away. Every choice you make starting today will have a positive or negative impact on how happy or unhappy you are in the future. Furthermore, if you let other people make the hard choices for you, I guarantee that you will get lost in the real world and end up living a life you don't like. We need to start by taking what I call a "self-inventory."

When a store performs an inventory check, it is reviewing and recording the different types of items in the store. This is done to see how much money the store has made, how well certain items have sold, and what it needs to order in the future. So, for the sake of this exercise, treat yourself like a store. Start to take an inventory of your life up to this point. Get an idea of where you are at in the parts and sections that matter the most when it comes to preparing for the rest of your life.

Following is a checklist to get you started. These questions are a result of the most common regrets and mistakes that were listed in the survey answers from the college graduates I questioned. Take 10–20 minutes and answer these questions as openly and honestly as you can.

Self-Inventory: Part 1

1. Do you study enough for your tests?
   - a. If no, why do you think that is?
   - b. If yes, what motivates you?
2. Did you/Do you try your best in high school?
   - a. If no, why do you think that is?
   - b. If yes, what motivates you?
3. Do you try your best in college? (If applicable)
   - a. If no, why do you think that is?
   - b. If yes, what motivates you?
4. What are your bad habits (e.g., rushing through homework, studying only the night before, copying friends' work, not paying attention in class)?
5. Can these affect your college prospects?
   - a. If you are already in college, do you think these bad habits affected your college prospects?
6. Can these affect your prospects in getting a job?
7. Are you trying to fix these habits?
   - a. If yes, is it working?
   - b. If no, why are you not trying/why is it not working?
8. What do you do on a daily basis that prepares you for being an adult?
9. What else should you be doing to prepare for the next steps in your life?

Congratulations! You just took the self-inventory. Did you answer them honestly? If not, go back and answer them honestly! Hopefully, by answering these questions, you began to understand where you need to start. Starting to become prepared means understanding where you are in life and what you need to work on. It also means to understand what faults and shortcomings are reasonable and which need to be addressed immediately. For example, if you are someone who studies hard but enjoys being lazy on the weekends, that is pretty typical. No need to be too hard on yourself there. However, if you are someone who is seeing high school and college as nothing more than a pointless obligation (like I did, and paid for it later!), that is a huge red flag.

You see, people seem to think that if you pass your classes, you are completely set. You're not.

If you treat high school as something you need to survive, then you won't get anything valuable out of it. Then, just when you think you are done with this pointless obligation, you are hit with a harder, longer, and more stressful commitment known as a full-time job. As you are looking at your answers try to see which ones may indicate issues in your attitude. Try to identify habits that may make your life as an adult harder. Remember, we are trying to create a long-term plan to live a fulfilling, joyful life.

Read back through all your answers. As you do this, look for any common themes. Do you see any similarities in your responses? Any problems that you can identify and start to fix? Take me for example. If I were to answer these questions when I was in high school, the common theme would have been laziness, procrastination, and doing just enough to get by. You see, people seem to think that if you pass your classes, you are completely set. You're not. You may "pass" according to your school's criteria, but if you did not learn anything and grow as a person, you might as well have gotten an F, because you failed at the only thing that matters. Anyway, back to me! My answers would have been in the vein of someone who did not take education seriously and thought he had plenty of time to "figure it out." If I had done this exercise 15 years ago, I would have seen that I was beginning to develop several bad habits centered around a lack of caring about my future and a strong desire to take the easy way out.

If you wait until you're an adult to care about being an adult, you'll miss out on the opportunities that can allow you to become to the type of adult you want to become.

I would have been surprised by this result. I was a good kid, never got in serious trouble, and had a lot of friends. People thought I was funny and smart. You can be a good person and have faults. You can develop bad habits that are beyond your control. It's okay to admit that at the age of 14, 16, or 18 years old you aren't thinking about anything other than hanging out with your friends and having fun. That doesn't make you a bad person; it makes you a typical teenager! Being that way is normal. No one is expecting you to develop a life plan and have the next 40 years planned out at the age of 16! However, too many young students don't even think about this type of stuff until 10 years later. If you wait until you're an adult to care about being an adult, you'll miss out on the opportunities that can allow you to become to the type of adult you want to become. You don't need to have all the answers right now, but you need to start asking about and caring about the critical questions.

The most important question I posed to you in the previous chapters was "What type of person do you want to become?". This is a question I will be asking repeatedly because if this book does nothing else, by the time you're done, I want you to have a firm answer to it. To begin answering this question, we need to continue with our self-inventory. In this section, we discuss joy and fulfillment. Take some time to think about and answer these questions. Your answers will be the foundation for that type of person and life you are going to start to build.

Self-Inventory: Part 2

1. What do you do in your everyday life that brings you joy?
2. When are you at your happiest?
3. I want to be the type of person who _____ on a daily basis.
4. If you could have any job in the world, what would it be? (This could be ANYTHING, I will explain why in a minute!)
5. What types of jobs are similar to the job you listed for question 4?
6. What do you want to be remembered for at the end of your life?

Hopefully, you took some time and thought about these answers. I would suggest copying those questions into a Word or Google document. Then, set a calendar reminder for every 6 months to answer those questions again. This helps to ensure you are in touch with your inner self and on track to becoming that person you are building in your mind. I also suggest doing the same thing with the series of questions in your self-inventory from a couple of pages earlier (Part 1). This will help to ensure that you are breaking those bad habits and preventing them from returning.

So, let's analyze these questions. Most people do not ask themselves these questions until they are much older, and it is too late. It's important to note here my reluctance to use the word "happy" when I talk about building a future for ourselves. I do this because, no matter what career you end up in, you will not always be happy. As mentioned in Chapter 1, any job you have will come with bad days and stressful times. Even if you love your job, you may find that you are at your happiest when you are with family and friends. It's okay to be happy when you are away from your job because you enjoy spending time with those you care about. What we are trying to avoid is the situation in which, because you hate your job, you are only happy in any circumstance that doesn't involve being at work. That's the type of life we are trying to avoid.

When you read through your answers, you should start to see a common theme. The theme should be what types of things in your life make you feel good and give you a sense of purpose. Again, let's use yours truly as an example. If I took the time to answer these questions, instead of finding ways to avoid doing hard work, I would have noticed that I enjoy helping and entertaining people. I also would have seen that I enjoy being creative and writing. Lastly, I would have eventually discovered that I am not the type of person who can sit at a desk all day, and that this fact should influence where I go to college and what major I choose. Instead, I thought I had time to "figure it out" and ended up in an office job, stuck at a desk for 8 hours a day.

Now, there is nothing wrong with a job that requires desk work, but it's not for everyone. Society tends to convince us that the best course of action is to go to college, get a "safe degree" with a set career path, and then take a "safe job" in a cubicle, with benefits, 401(k), and reasonable commuting time. This type of path is already laid out for you, and if you tend to be the uninspired, path-of-least-resistance type of student, then you could take this path and call it a day. However, I am warning you right now—you are going to regret it.

You will be much happier if you follow through on this self-inventory and create your own path. This path will more likely lead to a happy life, regardless of what society may think of it. If you start by taking this self-inventory and then implementing the results into your day-to-day routine, the end result will be a future and life that you will truly enjoy living.

You may not become exactly what you want, but if you can figure out why you want to have that "crazy" job, you can begin to identify what other jobs you can obtain that will bring you the same amount of joy.

Do you see a theme in your answers? Do you enjoy helping people? If you had a choice, would you entertain an audience, work with animals, or solve complex problems? What is that dream job that is rattling around in your head? Even if it's something like "baseball player" or "actress," that's fine. You may think it's crazy to think that way because "it will never happen" and it's "just a crazy dream." The truth is, the odds of becoming a baseball player or actress are slim. However—and this is crucial—you have to remember why you chose that in the first place. If you want to become a baseball player, it is because you love sports and love competing. Maybe playing in the MLB is not in the cards, but a future working in sports in some capacity is possible. It's not about becoming a ballplayer, it's about becoming the type of person who works every day with something that involves your passion, sports. You may not become exactly what you want, but if you can figure out why you want to have that "crazy" job, you can begin to identify what other jobs you can obtain that will bring you the same amount of joy.

As I mentioned, society tends to steer us down one path. It tends to want to keep us in a box. It's important to remember that there is nothing, literally nothing, that says you have to follow these types of rules and guidelines. If you do not want to work in an office, then you don't have to. If you do not want to go to college (more on that later) than you don't have to! The only thing you have to do is start to plan for your future. Start to decide the type of person you want to become, the life you want to lead, and the legacy you want to leave. Start to discover what kinds of jobs, careers, and industries excite you. Figure out what it is that you won't mind doing day in and day out for several years at a time. Then, begin to figure out what you have to do to get there.

At this point, we have begun taking a self-inventory, and we've begun building a solid foundation for the rest of your life. Again, do not feel like you have to have all the answers already.

You do not. This is merely an exercise to get your brain thinking a different way. To begin thinking long term instead of just in the moment. To start getting comfortable with thinking about the future and make the intentional decision to care about the next steps in your life. If you begin doing that, you are in pretty good shape.

I would also like you to start to identify two to three people in your life who can act as mentors. For those who do not know what a mentor is, think of it as someone whom you can ask questions of, seek advice from, and talk to about your concerns. A mentor will be able to advise you when you find yourself in a complex or challenging situation. It's essential to begin to create what I call your "mentorship circle." While this book will provide valuable overall advice, you will often find yourself seeking the counsel of those who know you best. I would suggest only including one parent in this circle. The reason I say this goes back to what I mentioned in Chapter 3. Their advice, while incredibly valuable, may at times be biased toward leading you down a safer path. Of course, you should go to your parents for advice, but remember that the final decision always rests with you. The other two people can be a mix of older relatives, teachers, professors, or family friends. These people may change over the years depending on where you are in your academic career. The bottom line is to start identifying those people in your life who you can help you achieve your goals. Begin to understand the importance of asking other people for their opinion to ensure you are making the most informed choices. There is nothing wrong with asking for help.

As I said, this book is going to cover a lot of ground and is designed to guide you through some of the most complex, exciting, and challenging years of your life. The upcoming chapters are going to walk you through 8 years of education, opportunities, choices, and situations. This book is truly meant to be a guidebook and instruction manual. With that said, before we dive into the wild world of high school and college, I want to help you create a plan. I want to create a game plan for how you are going to make the most out of the next six chapters of this book.

I want you to think of yourself as at the beginning of a journey. This may seem childish, but bear with me. This journey begins wherever you currently are in your educational career, and it ends with being an adult and starting your professional career. Remember, there are a lot of ways this journey can end. What I need you to do is to decide how you want it to end. What do you want that part of your life to look like? What does being a happy adult, working a job you enjoy, look like for you? What are you doing in this vision? Are you in a forest? On a stage? Are you helping children or animals? Maybe what you are doing is not clear, but you know it has something to do with technology, medicine, sports, or government. Whatever that vision is, lock in on it. It may change over time, but it's crucial to start thinking this way. To start envisioning what you want this part of your life to look like. Remember, your career takes over the majority of your time. Most people did not do what I am asking you to do, and they pretty much regret it every day.

When I talk to college graduates, they almost always tell me how they never really thought about what being an adult was going to be like. They did not think about the fact that what they did for a living would take up so much of their time. They never took the time to do the activities, ask the questions, and put in the work I am going to ask you to do in the coming chapters. The end result for many of those graduates was a life they never intended on living. So, while the next few chapters will require effort, it is all for a very important reason.

The reason I am so serious about this is because of what is at stake. I've seen firsthand what happens to people who did not take their education seriously.

Next, I want you to think about how you are going to utilize the information I am providing you in this book. You have an idea of what is coming in the next few chapters. You will be told what opportunities to take advantage of, what's important, what's not important, how to do research and network, what colleges are looking for, what employers are looking for, what past mistakes graduates have made, and more. How are you going to use this information to your benefit? How are you going to take this knowledge and apply it to your own personal journey? You see, I cannot do that part for you. I can share my thoughts and research. My friends and colleagues can dispense their advice and wisdom, but YOU are the one that has to do the work. If you are going to read this book and then put it on the shelf, you might as well stop reading now. This book will do you no good if you read it once and do nothing else. You have to take every story, statistic, and every piece of advice and apply it to your educational journey.

The reason I am so serious about this is because of what is

at stake. I've seen firsthand what happens to people who did not take their education seriously. People who didn't think about the future and then found themselves in a dull, joyless job, doing things that they had no desire in doing. They ended up living a life they never intended on living. That is my warning to you. The real world does not have to be awful, but it does need to be taken seriously.

So make the call. This train is leaving the station with or without you. What's the plan? Where do you want to end up when we are done? I would highly suggest reviewing the self-inventory questions I asked earlier in this chapter. Then I would write out as much detail as possible to describe the type of person you want to become. Once you know where you want to end up, you can start to figure out how to get there. Ready? Good! Next stop: high school.

Chapter 5:

Surviving High School

If you are currently a college student, you may feel as though this chapter does not pertain to you. I would highly suggest you read this chapter anyway. You may not have taken full advantage of your high school years. If you were like me, and many of the people I have surveyed, you did not try your hardest in high school. I know I didn't, and I ended up paying for it for years afterward. It's important to understand where you might have fallen short so you can make up for it moving forward. For anyone who is currently a post-high school student, feel free to use this chapter as a checklist of what you did and didn't do to prepare yourself for the real world.

For anyone who is in middle or high school, this chapter is designed to guide you, year by year, through the next 4 years. Later in this chapter, I am going to break each year down and provide you with a blueprint for making the most of your high school experience. Again, even if you are halfway done or more with high school, it is very much worthwhile checking out the plan and ensuring you are on the right track. This part of the book has something for everyone.

It's only until you become an adult that you realize that the "nerds" end up making all the money. It's about how smart you are now, not how cool you were back then.

When you are young, you tend to have a negative outlook and attitude toward school. It is seen as something you have to do and something you are not supposed to enjoy. It's cool to dislike school, and anyone seen otherwise is labeled as a nerd. It's only until you become an adult that you realize that the "nerds" end up making all the money. It's about how smart you are now, not how cool you were back then. Nevertheless, we are trained from an early age to dislike the idea of going to school. By the time you reach high school, you've been going to state-mandated classes for 8 years. It's easy to start getting tired of the monotony of going to class, sitting at a desk and learning topics that do not interest you. The key is to understand that starting now, it counts.

Don't get me wrong—all grade levels are essential. Elementary and middle school are crucial to your development as a child and a person. However, high school is different and needs to be treated as such. The choices you make in high school can positively or negatively affect the rest of your life. Everything you do in high school should give you the best possible chance to succeed in the future. Here's the problem: you have A LOT going on in high school. Education is just one of many things you have to juggle, and it's very easy to be so focused on what right is in front of you. Also, if you are unaware of what the real world is like, which we already established you probably are, then how are you supposed to be focused on your future? How are you supposed to know what opportunities to take advantage of?

High school comes at a bad time. Why? Because you are also going through puberty and becoming an adult. Now, I am absolutely not going to dive into the subject of puberty. Nope, not going to happen. However, I will sympathize with you and say this: when you are in high school, your body is changing, you are getting pimples you cannot control, your once-nice classmates are all becoming popular and mean, AND you're entering into a new educational phase during which you are supposed to start thinking about college and your life plans . . . and that is A LOT OF STUFF to handle. All these factors make high school the hardest schooling you will ever go through. It might not be the toughest curriculum you will have to learn, but it can be the toughest experience because of all the other worries you have going on at the same time. The important thing is to breathe. No really, take a breath.

I'm going to give you a piece of advice you are going to ignore. I know you are going to ignore it because almost everyone, me included, does. The advice is this: remember that most of the things you will worry about in high school are entirely pointless. They really are. The drama, tragedies, and heartbreak that seem to be overwhelming and catastrophic now have literally zero influence on the rest of your life. Yes, when they are happening, they are life consuming and yes, despite your best efforts, you will fall into the drama trap. It's fine. We all did it. It's kind of a rite of passage.

The thing to understand is that you need to focus on what is important. Focus on the things that *do* influence the rest of your life. Don't forget why you are in school. You are in school to get an education and better yourself. You are not just there to be with your friends or because you *have* to be. If you have that type of attitude, you will spend the next 4 years doing the bare minimum to get by and have very little show for it. Make your education a top priority and try your best to block out the rest of the noise (social media definitely included). Try and remember that what you are going through in these 4 years can determine your level of satisfaction for the next 40 years.

Think back to when we talked about the type of person you want to become. Hopefully, by now, you have the beginnings to the answer to that question. If not, I want you to take some time and try your best answer that question. Once you have an answer to that, I would like you to create a list of three to five jobs or careers that are associated with that type of person. I have included this helpful table to get your wheels turning.

Table 1. Sample Possible Jobs List

Type of Person	Obvious Careers	Less Obvious Careers
Healer	Doctor/Nurse/ Physician's Assistant	Psychologist, Nutritionist, Guidance Counselor, Chiropractor, Case Manager, Social Worker
Educator	Teacher	Instructor, Writer, Editor, Filmmaker, Researcher
Protector	Police Officer/ Firefighter	Corrections Officer, Cyber Security Technician, 911 Dispatcher, Security Installation Professional

Helper/ Advice Giver	Psychologist/ Psychiatrist	Guidance Counselor, Police Officer, Probation Officer, Social Worker, Case Manager
Athlete	Sports Anchor	Sports Writer, Sports Photographer, Sports-Themed Business Owner, Sports Producer

Have that list of possible careers handy. Keep in mind that your list can completely change. You may find yourself adding to this list or you may see yourself choosing a new person to become and having to start all over again. The important thing is that you have begun to think differently, and you are ready to make intentional choices that will lead to a purposeful life!

Before we dive into my year-by-year plan, I would like you to do one more thing. Remember earlier, when I asked you to make a list of everything your parents do for you? Did you make that list? Were you honest with yourself? Make sure you have that list as well, and make sure that it includes everything! This means cooking, cleaning, doing laundry, making doctors' appointments, driving you places, and anything else they do now but that you will have to be doing when you're an adult. That list will be needed as we move forward.

The following is a 4-year plan for high school. At the beginning of each section I have listed a set of goals. You may not understand them at first, but you will after you read through that section. Remember, everyone's journey is unique. I cannot possibly write out a plan that works perfectly for you. Nor will I walk you step-by-step through anything you are more than capable of doing on your own. For this to work, you need to take ownership of your education and your future. You have to want to achieve more and have a desire to become that person you are building in your head. You also have to accept that following this plan means a few things.

First, you will have to work harder. It will be tempting (and rather effortless) to do just enough to get by. Second, you will have to make difficult choices. Lastly, you may need to leave some people behind. What I mean by that is that when you decide to take control of your future, you may have friends who refuse to do the same. While they can remain your friends, you may find yourself traveling this road alone. You may be inside studying while they are out partying. They may still be in that "school is boring" mode while you are attending tutoring sessions and extracurricular activities. The sight of you succeeding may bother them, and it could cause issues. As you navigate the awkward situations, remember the end goal. Remember that life you want to build.

Okay, let's begin.

Freshman Year

Goals

1. Research the careers on your Possible Jobs List.
2. Create your LinkedIn profile.
3. Start a professional relationship with your guidance counselor.
4. Begin to develop strong study habits.
5. Research extracurricular activities that your school offers.

6. Start to work toward a 3.0+ GPA.

7. Begin to take over one activity your parents are doing for you.

When I list out goals such as these, I am itemizing things to accomplish that can help you make the most out of high school. I am also instructing you to do the very thing that my colleagues said they did *not* do. Lastly, I am pointing out what things are important to do, things you might not have realized were indeed important. These and the goals for your other school years are designed to keep you on track. I understand this might be a bit overwhelming right now, so we will tackle them one at a time, relate them to your freshman year, and discuss how they can positively impact the rest of your life.

1. Research the careers on your Possible Jobs List.

Before you even step foot in high school, the first thing I would like you to do is list out the three to five possible jobs that came as a result of answering the question of the type of person you want to become. Remember, the list can change, but you should have a pretty good idea of what jobs are going to help you develop that long-lasting, fulfilling career. The reason I want you to have the list ready is that this is the time to start exploring. Freshman year is the time to start researching these jobs and determining whether they are a good fit for you.

Begin by looking into what type of schooling you will need. What types of majors do people in these professions usually study? What is the average salary, and what does the day-to-day workload look like? You may want to ask yourself whether you even need to go to college to obtain these jobs. We are going discuss the decision to go to college (or not) in the next chapter. However, this is the time to see whether your passion is aligned with college or whether you should begin exploring trade schools and other avenues of education. Regardless, you need to understand what the jobs and careers are like so you can avoid being blindsided and forced into a life you don't want.

2. Create your LinkedIn profile.

Online research of your passions and possible jobs will only get you so far. If you want to gain a well-rounded understanding, you need to seek out those who are currently doing the jobs you want to be doing. They will have the answers to the questions you are asking. First, ask around your inner circle of family and friends. Make your ambitions known and see whether anyone knows someone in the field of study you're interested in. Next, reach out to industry professionals and high school alumni via LinkedIn. When you connect with these professionals, ask them direct questions such as what their day-to-day work routine is like, what they like about the profession, what they don't like about the profession, what they studied in school, what they know now about the job that they did not know then, and what would they have done differently. This is the information you need to make informed choices and prepare for the next steps in your life.

Now, if you are a high school freshman, you may not know what LinkedIn is, and if you do, you most likely do not have a LinkedIn profile. This is totally fine. Most "experts" will say that you can wait until college to do this. However, if you haven't noticed by now, we don't "wait," we prepare! Creating an account is pretty simple. Be sure to use a friendly, professional looking photograph to use as your profile picture. Do not be stressed by not have a long list of work experience. Just list your high school as your current employer and "high school student" as your current role. Under the headline, just write what you are doing—for example, "Current high school student actively seeking knowledge to prepare for college and the real world." No expects a high school student to have a long working history. In fact, most working professionals you come across will be impressed that you are taking the time to create this professional presence and are interested in seeking out their opinions.

3. Start a professional relationship with your guidance counselor.

Another individual who can assist in your future career research is your school guidance counselor. In your first month, take a trip to the guidance counselor's office and meet him or her in person. During your first meeting, talk about your plan, goals, and the future jobs you are considering. It is entirely likely that your counselor will be able to share resources with you or connect you with working professionals and past alumni. Regardless, begin to develop a relationship with this important person. Do not be discouraged if he or she cannot find the time for you immediately. These individuals are often overworked and tasked with helping juniors and seniors find and apply to colleges. Your time will come, but for now, it is important that your counselor knows who you are and what you are looking to accomplish.

It is your responsibility that you study hard, ask the right questions, do the proper research, and gain a complete understanding of what is going to be expected of you in college.

As important as this relationship is, you cannot count on your guidance counselor or school to do all the hard work for you. Nothing against your school—there are a lot of students with a lot of needs. According to a study done by the National Assessment of Educational Progress, 46% of high school students feel school has adequately prepared them for what careers match their interests and abilities, and 40% of students felt that school had done a poor or fair job of helping them understand what knowledge and skills they needed for college success. Lastly, an astounding 80% of high school students said they would have tried harder if their school had set higher expectations.

What all that data tells me is that students are falling into the bad habit of assuming that high school is going to teach them everything they need to know. This is simply not true. While your school and education will open up opportunities for you, it is up to you to ensure you are doing what needs to be done. It is your responsibility that you study hard, ask the right questions, do the proper research, and gain a complete understanding of what is going to be expected of you in college.

4. Begin to develop strong study habits.

This goal may look like an obvious one to most students.

Developing solid study habits may seem like a given, but I cannot tell you how many college graduates I have spoken with regret not studying more in school. In the survey that I sent them, the most common answer to questions about regret include lack of studying. If you do a quick internet search of "high school students regret not studying more," you will see several links to articles and messages boards filled with grads saying the same thing over and over again. The reason they are filled with such regret is because it ended up hurting them in ways they could not predict when they were younger.

According to data collected by the National Assessment of Educational Progress, only 37% of high school graduates are prepared for college-level math and science courses. That number is alarmingly low and clearly states that the status quo strategy is not going to cut it if you want to be ready for college-level work. Another alarming stat from the same report stated that 43% of students entering a 2-year school and 23% of students entering a 4-year school were forced to take remedial courses because they failed a college-readiness assessment after being accepted. This means that before they can start college classes that count toward graduation, they have to retake what they did not learn in high school. That is just a waste of time.

This is why so many graduates struggle when they enter the workforce. They never developed strong work habits. They never learned how to do more than just enough. They never taught themselves to exceed expectations.

I know I personally did not study nearly as much as I should have. Why? Because my goal for every test was to pass. I treated high school and the corresponding work as something I had to survive. It was something I had to get through on a daily basis. I never made the connection to how today's math test will impact my chances of getting into college, and how my choice of college affects my career prospects. I, and so many former students like me, was very nearsighted in my approach to studying. If the topic did not interest me, or if I had something better to do, I just studied enough to get a decent grade or not get in trouble with my parents. This is why so many graduates struggle when they enter the workforce. They never developed strong work habits. They never learned how to do more than just enough. They never taught themselves to exceed expectations.

What exactly do I mean by strong study habits? When I talk about study habits, I talk about ensuring that studying, homework, and all other kinds of schoolwork are given the proper place in your life. Do not treat your education as something you are forced to endure. Do not do what I did and treat high school like a social hour and school assignments like obstacles to dodge and survive in a video game. Choose to make your education the center of your life for the next 4 years.

This will not be the popular thing to do. You will have friends who will try and convince you that school is for losers and being social is much more important. You may have family who will try to convince you that school is a waste of time and that the real world is going to be awful regardless of what you do. You have to be stronger than that. You have to mentally create that life you want to live, place it in the center of your vision, and lock into it. This is why choosing a purpose, passion, and career is so important. It will pick you up during the tough times and give you the encouragement you need to soldier on. You are building a life you want to live. You will end up happy and fulfilled, even if your friends and family won't.

Identify which courses are your strengths and which are your weaknesses. This is a practice you will be going through for years to come. This practice is essential to understanding where you need to spend your time studying and how much time you need to carve out for each subject. If you determine that you are in danger of struggling in a subject, don't avoid it, attack it. Put together a plan that includes extra help, a tutor, and more studying time. It is entirely possible that this topic will have nothing to do with your future. The trap is that most people think such a subject, one that surely won't have anything to do with your future, means it is a waste of time and should be ignored. Grade point averages don't work like that. Your GPA, which we will break down in coming sections, incorporates all of your grades. This might not be fair, but it is the game you have to play to get into a good college.

As previously mentioned, strong study habits go beyond just studying for tests. They also include attention to homework and projects. Homework in itself is an uphill battle. The content might not be challenging, but the circumstance surrounding it can be. Homework is done typically at the end of the day. After you have been in class for 6–7 hours, being lectured on topics that may have been less than exciting, you now have to sit down and do more work. Not to mention, it's designed to be done once you are home, when all you want to do is watch TV and play video games. A reluctance to want to do homework does not make you lazy, it makes you human! It's not always about what you want to do but instead about what you need to do. Not only does homework need to be done but it also needs to be done to the best of your ability (and not because everything you learn is going to be used in your future profession). You need to try your hardest when completing homework because you want to start building that habit of completing tasks and projects to the best of your ability.

5. Research extracurricular activities that your school offers.

Once you have started to create a plan to excel during the school day, you should be moving on to what you do after school. Of course, your studies should come before anything else, because, as we showed, they are the backbone of your plan to build your ideal life. As mentioned previously, if you are struggling in any subject, you owe it to yourself to get extra help so your GPA does not suffer. With all that being said, you will still have a decent amount of free time to work with. This ties into what we were discussing earlier about deciding what type of person you want to become and, more importantly, the type of life you want to live. Do you want to be the type of person who does just enough to get by? Someone who can't wait to leave school, run home, and play video games? You should want to be more than that. Freshman year is the year to start to become a person who aspires to be more than ordinary. Start to understand that if you are going to build the life you want, you have to start putting in the time and effort in ways others won't. One of the many ways you can do this is to take advantage of the after-school clubs and organizations your high school offers.

Getting involved in extracurricular activities is highly beneficial for three main reasons. First, you are starting to explore options and possibilities outside your comfort zone. You already have an idea of what you like and what you are good at. Now, begin to explore other topics and interests. Start to see whether it's possible that you have talents and skills you never even knew about. This is also a great way to start surrounding yourself with like-minded people. You can begin to build new friendships with other students who are as motivated and hardworking as you are. These types of friendships will become invaluable as you start to navigate the obstacles in high school and need someone to motivate you along the way.

The second reason for getting involved is the positive impact it will have on your college application process. Extracurriculars are something that college admissions officers look at. They want to see how much time and effort you put into school. They also want to know if you are a well-rounded, hardworking student, with many things to offer their college community. Extracurricular involvement can also demonstrate your loyalty and leadership skills. If you join a club freshman year and stick with it for 4 years, it shows admissions officers that you are willing to work with a team until the end. You can also use those experiences to point out how you have developed into a leader and talk about specific instances in which you used your leadership skills to solve problems. These types of clubs send a clear message that you are serious about being as smart and prepared as possible for college and the real world.

Lastly, taking on this type of commitment helps with your

time management. For example, if you go straight home every day from school, you will probably walk through the door around 3–4 pm. Assuming you are not going to bed until 10–11 pm, that leaves about 7 hours to study and do your homework. Having that much time may seem appealing, but it could very well work against you. You may lack the motivation to get started because you feel as though you have plenty of time. If you are not getting home until 5 or 6 pm and cannot begin your homework until after dinner, you will feel more pressure to use that time wisely. Studies show that those students who have less time to mess around end up getting better grades. Furthermore, as we mentioned in Chapter 2, when we broke down the hours of your week, you are headed toward a life of more work time than free time. You are better off preparing yourself for that type of lifestyle by filling your hours with productive tasks that make you more prepared as opposed to pointless tasks that do not yield any tangible results.

Time management is also a crucial skill to start building up for college. The Student Engagement Insight Survey asked 3,004 college students: "Do you struggle with time management?" An overwhelming majority, 78%, of respondents said they sometimes struggle with this, with an additional 9% saying they often struggle with it. Again, these numbers show that many students are not prepared to manage their own time in college. It is important to do more than what is being asked of you, in order to find yourself among the 13% who said they never struggle with this issue.

6. Start to work toward a 3.0+ GPA.

Next, I want to talk about something that I never gave

much thought to when I was in high school—your grade point average, or GPA. If you are unfamiliar with this, it is basically an average of all of your grades. A couple of things be aware of: first, in this system, all grades are treated equally. For example, let's say that you are great at English and know that it will be a part of your future. Those grades are counted as equally as your grades for subjects you cannot stand and know you will never use again. This is something to keep in mind when you need to study for a test in a subject you do not like. That being said, I would challenge any freshman to work toward a 3.0 GPA by the end of their freshman year. By setting this goal, you are giving purpose to every test, project, essay, and homework assignment. As I said earlier, you may not like history or think you will ever use algebra again, but a bad grade can hurt your GPA. A series of bad grades in the same subject can harm your GPA enough that it can hurt your chances of getting into the college you want. If you ever need the motivation to study more for a test or work harder on a project, think about the type of person you want to become. Imagine that career and life you are building in your head. Be the type of person who is willing to go through a little pain now to avoid a lifetime of pain and stress later.

7. Begin to take over one activity your parents are doing for you.

Lastly, before we move onto sophomore year, I have one last task for you, and it has nothing to do with your education. Remember that list of things your parents are currently doing for you? I want you to take one item off that list and commit to doing it for yourself. The easiest one may be doing your own laundry. By doing this, you are starting to prepare yourself for adulthood and all the responsibilities you will have to take on. It is possible your mom or dad may push back say it's not necessary or insist that there's "a system." I would just gently remind your parents that you are trying to prepare yourself for the real world and that this is a part of your plan. The key is, once you take over this task, you cannot go back. This is something you are committed to doing from here on out.

Sophomore Year

Goals

1. Calculate your GPA; ensure it is above a 3.0.
2. Conduct your first Internal Educational Audit.
3. Research when the appropriate time is to start looking at colleges.
4. Begin to plan for how you are going to pay for college.
5. Begin meeting with your guidance counselor on a monthly basis.
6. Identify one person in your life to become a possible mentor.
7. Confirm your choices on your Possible Jobs List.
8. Take over a second activity your parents are doing for you.

Now we have moved on to sophomore year. It is my personal opinion that this becomes a lost year, and for some students, a "trap year." What I mean is that the other three years in your high school education have a specific meaning. When you are a freshman, everything is new and exciting. When you are a junior, you start looking at colleges, and when you are a senior, you pick a college. It will be easy to fall into the trap that most students fall into and just coast through this year. Not you! You can't do this, because you have a plan to follow!

1. Calculate your GPA; ensure it is above a 3.0.

First, sit down before your sophomore year starts and calculate your GPA from your freshman year to confirm it is at least a 3.0. It is possible that this information could be available through your school, but I advise calculating it yourself. This gives you a chance to look at all of your grades and understand where your strengths and weaknesses are. It's very possible that you will see a pattern emerging. Your best grades were in the classes you cared the most about and were most interested in. Your lower grades were in classes you found boring, difficult, or frustrating.

This gives us two valuable pieces of insight. First, you can start to determine what you enjoy learning and doing. Start figuring out what satisfies you and how it aligns with the type of person you want to become. How do the classes you enjoy fit into the possible jobs you have listed out? Second, you are starting to identify where your challenges are going to be. As I said, if you are not careful, the classes you deem as boring can have a negative impact on your future plans. This is the time settle in and declare that you are going to try your hardest in every class because your future depends on it. You may not like history, but you should like preparing for the future. You may not like math, but you should like the type of life you are trying to build.

2. Conduct your first Internal Educational Audit.

Your sophomore year is also when you will conduct your first Internal Educational Audit. This is an exercise designed to understand where you are in your educational journey and ensure that you are on the path to building a life that you love. Below is a template for this audit, but feel free to add in anything else you think is relevant. Remember, you are in charge of this journey. Copy this into a Word document or notepad. I would advise reviewing these questions before the start of every school year.

Internal Educational Audit

1. What is your current GPA?
    a. What class did you get your best grade in?
    b. What class did you get your worst grade in?
2. What was your favorite class and why?
3. What was your least favorite class and why?
4. What are three things you learned when you researched your Possible Jobs List?
5. Is your Possible Jobs List still the same or has it changed? Why?
6. Do you have a better idea of the type of life you want to live now than you did when you started the school year last year?
7. What did you do last year to make yourself a more attractive college applicant?
8. Did you study as much as you could for every test? If not, why do you think that is?

You are going to revisit this template at the beginning of each school year. However, for now, this should give you an idea of whether you did what you needed to do during your freshman year. If you end up falling short, that is okay. However, it is better to understand where your areas for improvement are now, instead of 10 years from now when you are in the real world struggling to understand why your career isn't going so great. If you are reading this before your sophomore year, feel free to copy it down and look at it every once in a while. If you know you are going to have to answer these questions at some point, it may motivate you to produce the answers you are going to want to write down.

3. Research when the appropriate time is to start looking at colleges.

Most students will not start thinking about colleges until next year. Again, that's not you, because you are prepared! I am not going to tell you when the appropriate time to start looking at colleges is. Why? Because you need to start doing things like this on your own. That type of information is readily available. It's my job to give you advice, tasks, and wisdom that you can't find on the internet. With that being said, begin to understand when you need to start looking at colleges, scheduling campus visits, and looking at financial aid options. This is also a time to start talking to your parents about how you plan on paying for college.

4. Begin to plan for how you are going to pay for college.

I want to stop for a minute and emphasize the importance

of figuring out how you are going to pay for college. The reason I am zeroing in on this is because of the results from the survey I sent out to many college graduates. In one way or another, almost all the participants talked about not fully understanding their student loans or wishing they had chosen a cheaper college. Furthermore, student loan debt is a significant reason why so many people are miserable at their jobs and living unfulfilling, stressful lives. Allow me to explain.

College is expensive. You could make the argument that it is too expensive, but that is a different conversation for another time. It is not going to change any time soon, so you have to work with what you are given. Most people take out student loans to cover some or all of the cost of college. What many of my friends, coworkers, and survey respondents did not look into was the interest rates attached to those loans. When you take out a loan, you not only have to pay that money back but you also have to pay it back *with interest*. In simple terms, you are paying back more than you borrowed. Think about it—why would a bank give you thousands of dollars unless there was something in it for them? Many students pick a college without thinking about the long-term ramifications of the cost. They take out a loan and figure they can think about it later. While this may work in the beginning, and you are essentially getting an immediate education without having to pay anything, there is going to be a massive bill waiting for you when you graduate. Once you enter into the real world, you are expected to start paying back your loan on a monthly basis. This monthly payment could be as small as $100 per month or as large at $1,000 per month depending on where you went to school, how big your loan was, and whether you received your master's degree along with your bachelor's.

A sizeable monthly payment like this, on top of additional adult bills such as rent, cell phone, cable/internet, and grocery shopping can put a severe strain on your happiness and well-being. It may also restrict you from doing the things you really enjoy in life. This also plays into my point earlier about being restricted from changing careers. If you spend several years in one industry or profession, you may not be able to go back and restart your career because you will not be able to afford that type of salary reduction.

Just like all the other points and facts in this book, I do not say this to scare you or deter you from going to an expensive school or taking out loans. I say this so you can avoid the mistakes that so many students who came before you have made. Talk to your parents about paying for college and determine how much they will be helping you or whether you are going to require loans to pay for all of it. This will allow you to have an estimate of how much money you have to start with. Next, understand how interest rates work. Do some research on student loans, when they need to be paid back, the difference between state and federal loans, and figure out what might work best for you. Then, when you start to look at colleges—understand how much they cost and why. We are going to dive more deeply into this in the rest of this chapter and next chapter, but it is essential to understand why a college costs as much as it does. Lastly, keep all these numbers in mind when researching those potential jobs and what type of education is needed for each of them.

You should start to notice that everything we are talking about is starting to connect together to help you be as prepared as possible for college and the real world. Don't worry; we have an entire chapter on the college selection process coming up. That chapter will include a checklist for when it comes time to applying for those student loans.

5. Begin meeting with your guidance counselor on a monthly basis.

Sophomore year is also the time to strengthen your relationship with your guidance counselor. Begin to have monthly meetings with him or her and ensure you are on the right track. It may help motivate you to stay on top of your studies if you know you have to report your progress every month. These meetings are also a great time to talk about those potential jobs you have been researching. Remember, the key is to connect with people who are currently doing those jobs. Your guidance counselor is a great resource to help you seek out and connect with these people. You counselor is also an ideal sounding board for your questions and concerns regarding student loans and the cost of college. Lastly, these types of relationships will be invaluable when it comes time to apply to colleges that require letters of recommendation from school staff.

6. Identify one person in your life to become a possible mentor.

Your next goal is to find a mentor. This one is tricky, and here is why: a mentor is someone who is experienced enough to guide you through various challenges and knowledgeable enough to give you advice when you need it. This is someone you can learn a great deal from just because they have already experienced what you have gone through and can help you chart the best path possible. However, not everyone can be a mentor. A mentor is someone who has the time and energy to guide you. It is also someone you feel a deep connection to. You cannot merely pick a mentor out of a lineup. It's something that has to happen organically.

Start to look at the people in your life. Examine the relationships with your family, friends, and high school teachers. Is there someone whose opinion you value and you feel a special connection with? Did you have a teacher last year whom you liked more than most and felt like he or she understood you and your goals? If yes, then start to create a relationship with that person. Actively seek out this person's advice and then listen to what he or she has to say and put it into action. Like I said before, the answers to your questions usually lie with those who came before you. If you are lucky enough to meet someone who can help you succeed in life, make it a point to seek out that person's opinion and ask questions. It is the only way you can be sure you are making the best choice possible.

7. Confirm your choices on your Possible Jobs List.

Before the sophomore year ends, you will need to confirm the jobs listed on your Possible Jobs List. Ideally, you have done enough research and networking to narrow it down to two to three jobs. You are likely going to have to start looking at colleges in your junior year. That process will be made easier if you know what career you are looking to go into. Also, going back to the point about loans and costs, if you understand how much you will make in that career, you can compare that to the cost of the degree you will need. It is okay if your desired career does not make a lot of money right away, but you will want to avoid the stress of having to pay a hefty monthly student loan payment with a small entry-level salary.

Lastly, when you start to think about the type of career and life you want to build toward, it will give you even more motivation to study for your tests and do well in all of your classes, even the ones you don't like that much. Remember, you may not like math or science, but you should like the idea of living a life of joy and fulfillment instead of stress and regret.

8. Take over a second activity your parents are doing for you.

Finally, we come back to that list of chores your parents currently do for you. By now, you should have completely mastered the first one you took over in freshman year. I suggested laundry previously because it's the easiest one to learn. However, we need to keep this train moving. We need to start getting used to being an adult, so it doesn't smack us in the face when we graduate. Therefore, I challenge you to take over another item on that list. This time I suggest making your own lunches. This teaches you time management in the morning and gets you used to do something now when you have free time that you will eventually have to do anyway. You may think this is a small, pointless exercise, but you are preparing yourself for being an adult and being on your own. Taking care of yourself and your individual needs teaches you responsibility and discipline. It also allows you to make mistakes and slowly learn how to become an adult instead of trying to do everything on your own and all at once.

Junior Year

Goals

1. Complete research of all positions listed on Possible Jobs List.
2. Choose the job and/or career you want to pursue.
3. Conduct your second Internal Educational Audit.
4. Complete the Is College for Me? questionnaire.

We have now reached junior year. The next chapter is dedicated to the college selection process. When you enter your junior year, you will want to review this section AND the next chapter at the same time. The goals listed above are for you to get an idea of what this time of your life is going to be like. Nevertheless, when you reach your junior year, you should have the mindset of being prepared to focus on choosing the right college for you, your goals, and your budget.

1. Complete research of all positions listed on Possible Jobs List.

Before junior year begins, you must complete two essential tasks. First, make sure all research regarding the jobs on your Possible Jobs List is completed. You should understand the day-to-day tasks of each job, the starting and average salaries, what type of education you will need, and what those individuals currently in those jobs have to say about pursuing that type of career. If possible, you should try and spend some time during your summer break investigating at least one of these jobs. This could be in the form of a formal internship or just spending a few hours shadowing someone who has that job, seeing what the daily tasks are like. This isn't going to give you a full picture and will not be available for every type of job, but it is important always to be finding ways to understand what your career is going to be like. This is the only way to be prepared for your life when you enter the real world.

2. Choose the job and/or career you want to pursue.

The second task is to choose your desired job/career. As we said, you have done your research and understood what goes into this type of career. You know how much it pays and how that will affect your short- and long-term goals in life. You also understand the schedule you will have to work and what type of education you will need. By choosing your desired job now, you can select a college that offers you the correct major. You can also anticipate how much money you will make once you graduate and how much of a student loan you can afford. This will make you laser focused when researching and visiting colleges. You have taken out the guesswork and have a clear understanding of what type of major you are looking for and how much college you can afford.

It is important to remember that this choice you are making does not have to be permanent. You can change your mind as you grow throughout college. At this point you may still be interested in a couple different career paths. That is fine. The point of this goal is not to lock you into a choice for the rest of your life. The point is to simply motivate you to make a decision about your career interests so you have something to base your college choices on.

3. Conduct your second Internal Educational Audit.

You are also going to conduct your second Internal

Educational Audit before you start your junior year. I cannot stress enough the importance of self-responsibility. If you are going to build the life you want, then you must hold yourself accountable. It will be incredibly easy to fall back into bad habits, doing just enough to get by. Chances are, the people around you will be doing that already. Below I have re-listed the Internal Educational Audit for you, with a few slight tweaks. Again, be completely honest and use these answers to guide you through your upcoming school year.

Internal Educational Audit

1. What is your current GPA?
    a. What class did you get your best grade in?
    b. What class did you get your worst grade in?
2. What was your favorite class and why?
3. What was your least favorite class and why?
4. What were the three most important things you learned when you researched your Possible Jobs List?
5. Why did you choose the job you did from your Possible Jobs List?
6. Do you have a better idea of the type of life you want to live now than you did when you started the previous school year?
7. What did you do last year to make yourself a more attractive college applicant?
8. Did you study as much as you could for every test? If not, why do you think that is?
9. What major are you planning on studying in college and why?
10. What parts of the college selection process are you unsure about, and what steps will you take to better understand them?

4. Complete the Is College for Me? questionnaire.

A lot of what we have talked about so far has been built on the notion that you are going to go to college. Most people do end up going to college, and the majority of careers out there require some college degree. That being said, college is not for everyone, and one can have a long-lasting and lucrative career in a field that does not require a college degree. It is entirely possible that in the course of your research you may have discovered that the career you seek does not require a college education.

We are going to talk about trade schools and college alternatives in the next chapter, but if you currently find yourself questioning whether you should go to college or whether you have selected a career that does not require it, feel free to take this short Is College for Me? questionnaire.

Is College for Me?

1. Do the jobs on your Possible Jobs List require a college degree?

2. Do you find it difficult to sit at a desk for an extended amount of time?

3. Do you find enjoyment in working with your hands, being outside, or completing detail-oriented labor-intensive jobs?

4. Does learning a trade (e.g., health care technician, beautician, carpenter, electrician, plumber, auto mechanic, etc.) interest you more than engaging in the corporate/business world, perhaps sitting in front of a computer for long stretches?

5. Is the only reason you are considering college because you think you have to?

This not a quiz and there is no formula to decide whether college is for you. It is a choice you have to make on your own. Remember that you do not have to go to college if you don't want to. College is not for everyone. Don't get tricked into thinking that college is the only logical next step and the only way to make a living in this world. There are plenty of successful people who never got a college degree.

However, if you choose to forgo college, you need to have a plan. You need to still choose what career you want and understand what steps you need to take to achieve it. Simply taking a job after high school and adapting a "figure it out later" attitude is not going to work. You may find yourself working a dead-end job with no way to save money for your future. If you are not going to college, then you need to determine what career you want and be sure that it will be able to support you and the goals you have for your life.

As you know already, I went to college so my knowledge in the area of alternatives is limited. Unfortunately, unlike a lot of other aspects of being prepared for the real world, this is a subject on which I won't be as helpful. So, if you are starting to think that college is not for you, your next step is to connect with people who did not go to college either. Be sure you're talking to people who have gone on to successful careers. Get advice from people who still made something of themselves and avoid talking to those who were simply too lazy to go to college. There is a big difference.

5. Take over a third activity your parents were doing for you.

Following with the theme of the previous 2 years, I now

challenge you to take over a third item from your list of things your parents are currently doing for you. At this point, I would challenge you to really think hard about this one. Choose something personal and something that you know is important to start doing for yourself. Remember: think about what you will be forced to do for yourself when you are older. What should you start doing now to make your life easier when that day arrives? In addition to that task, I want you to take over a bonus task! This bonus task is setting an alarm and waking yourself up every day, if you are not doing so already. It also includes getting yourself out of bed and out the door on time. If you already do this, then great. If you don't, it will be much easier to start now and stumble a few times in high school than to wait for college and miss a class, or even worse, a test.

The rest of your junior-year goals, focused on selecting a college, will be covered in the next chapter. I would advise you to read this chapter and the next one in the same sitting the first time around. Then, as you move through high school and actually arrive at your junior year, you can flip between this section and the next chapter.

Senior Year

Goals
1. Calculate your current GPA.
2. Conduct your third Internal Educational Audit.
3. Conduct your first Internal Personal Audit.
4. Learn about student loans and interest rates.

5. Apply to college/plan your next post-high school steps (covered in Chapter 6).

6. Finish all your classes by studying hard and improving your GPA.

7. Take over a fourth activity your parents are doing for you.

You have arrived at your last year of high school. At this point, you should have 3 years of hard work and preparation under your belt. You should feel confident about the next steps in your life because you did the research necessary to be prepared. You have spent the last 3 years figuring out what type of person you want to become and what type of life you want to build. Every decision you made was done to become that person and create that life. Before entering senior year, you should have an idea of the career you want to have, what major(s) you need to pursue, and a solid idea of what college you will be attending. If you have discovered and determined that college is not for you, your senior year is your chance to explore the various options that are open to you and start to build out your post-high school plan.

The term that is often associated with your senior year of high school is "senioritis." This term is referring to the feeling many high school students feel in their senior year. They fall into a trap, thinking that the hard part is over and that the second half of senior year is a piece of cake. It is treated as something you must go through before you enter college. This type of trap is precisely what has happened to countless students who have come before you. It is imperative that you remove this type of thinking before the year even starts. Also, you must never let this type of thinking enter into your brain again. From here on out, everything you do holds importance, and everything you do will affect your future. Nevertheless, you will be surrounded by those who will slack off and adopt a carefree attitude toward senior year. Stay focused building toward the life you have spent the last 3 years imagining.

1. Calculate your current GPA.

Just like we did at the beginning of the last 2 years, calculate your GPA. Is it high enough to apply to those colleges you were looking at? If not, what else about your application is going to make up for that? Also, remember that colleges reserve the right to review your transcript at the end of your senior year, regardless of whether they have accepted you. In blunt terms, if your GPA plummets because you stopped caring, you could be rejected from the very school that accepted you. Plus, you always want to be striving to improve your GPA because, in the event you are going on to college, you should be continually trying to improve your study habits. Your high school GPA might soon become irrelevant, but the work ethic you created will grow more relevant than ever over the coming years.

2. Conduct your third Internal Educational Audit.

Just like the pre-year calculation of your GPA, you should now, ideally, be using your final days of summer vacation to perform your third Internal Educational Audit. It is essential to understand that when you conduct this specific audit, there is not a lot you can do to improve on any negative answers you may come up with. What I mean is that you should have been fixing any issues that were coming out of your previous two audits. This audit should do two things: confirm you are ready for the next steps in your life and give you a solid understanding of what happened in high school.

Here is your final Internal Educational Audit, with some tweaks based on the fact that you are nearing the end of high school.

Internal Educational Audit

1. What is your current GPA?

    a. What subject did you get your best grades in?

    b. What subject did you get your worst grades in?

2. What was your favorite topic overall and why?

3. What was your least favorite topic overall and why?

4. What were the three most important things you learned when you researched colleges?

5. What colleges are on your shortlist and why?

6. Do you have a better idea of the type of life you want to live now than you did when you started the school year last year?

7. What did you do last year to make yourself a more attractive college applicant?

8. Are your study habits where they need to be in order to deal with the workload that comes with college level courses?

9. What habits do you need to improve on this year before you enter college?

3. Conduct your first Internal Personal Audit.

In addition to your Internal Educational Audit, I would now like you to conduct your very first Internal Personal Audit. This can be done at any point during your senior year, but ideally before you graduate. You will notice that this audit will have similar questions to the audits I will be asking you to conduct in the next chapter. It is important you treat these questions seriously and answer each series separately. The key to making the best choices for your future is to be fully aligned with and aware of who you are, where you are headed, your strengths, your weaknesses, and the type of life you need to live to be happy.

Following is the first Internal Personal Audit. I would suggest setting aside 30-60 minutes to really think about these questions and your answers. They can be as long and detailed as possible. This is also designed for any time in your life that you feel like you might be slipping off course.

Internal Personal Audit

1. What about your future are you most excited about?
2. What about your future are you least excited about?
3. What about post-high school life concerns you the most?
   a. What are you going to do address these concerns?
4. What about being adult and working full time concerns you the most?
   a. What are you going to do address these concerns?
5. What are you most proud of regarding your time in high school?
6. What regrets do you have regarding your time in high school?
   a. What are you going to do to ensure you do not regret the same things after college?
7. What are your three strongest attributes?
8. What are your three biggest weaknesses?
   a. What are you going to do to improve your weaknesses?

9. Can you honestly say you have done everything possible to be prepared for the real world?

    a. If no, where did you fall short, why is that, and what will you do to fix this?

This audit is designed for you to give yourself an honest picture of where you stand on your journey to becoming the person you want to become. You have to hold yourself accountable. No one in this world is going to care about your success more than you do. You may have supporters, mentors, and friends, but they also have their own lives to worry about. They are focused on their personal goals. You need to be focused on where you are headed at all times. It will always be tempting to take a step back, take a break, and adapt that "figure it out later" attitude. It takes a certain level of motivation and determination to keep pushing forward and keep wanting more for yourself and your future. That is why it is vital to take self-inventory-type tests such as this one and to answer them openly and honestly. Only then can you be sure that you are on the right path and be prepared for any issues that may pop up in the future.

4. Learn about student loans and interest rates.

As we have discussed, senior year is the time when you finally select the colleges you will be applying to. However, before we get there, I implore you to put aside some time at the beginning of the year to understand student loans and interest rates. In sophomore year, I stressed the importance of understanding how you are going to pay for college. By this point, you should understand how much money, if anything, you are getting from family. You should have a pretty good idea of how much college or trade school is going to cost because you have done your research and have a short list of schools you are going to apply to. We will cover the cost of college and what to look for in the next chapter. For now, I want to discuss the importance of understanding the loans you will likely be signing up for.

As previously mentioned, a student loan essentially entails you borrowing money from a bank. The bank is not giving you this money as a gift. They are giving you the money with interest, meaning that you will pay them back more than they gave you. The longer you take to pay them back, the more interest they will collect and the more money you end up paying them. No one expects you to be able to afford college on your own, so it is reasonable to take out this type of loan. However, you want to be sure you fully understand how much money you are going to owe after college. Specifically: when you have to start paying it back, how much you will be required to pay back per month, and for how long.

Here are a few questions to answers when looking at each student loan you are considering:

Pre-loan Checklist

1. What is the total amount of money I am borrowing?
2. What is the interest rate on this loan?
3. What is the total amount of money I will owe after college/trade school?
4. When will I have to start paying this loan back?
5. How much per month will I be required to pay?
6. If I only pay the minimum, how long will it take to pay back?

7. If I only pay the minimum, how much money in interest alone will I be paying?

8. Would this minimum amount be less if I chose a different school? How much less would it be?

9. Does this loan get deferred if I go to graduate school (if applicable)?

10. Do the terms of my first job affect the terms of my loan in any way?

11. Is it possible my loan could be forgiven or reduced if I enter into a specific job or industry?

If this type of research and questioning seems extreme to you, I understand. Most students apply for student loans without asking these questions. They assume they have no choice but to take out these loans and will figure the rest out after graduation. Here is the problem that they end up facing: they end up graduating with massive monthly payments. Depending on the interest rate, the number of loans, and the amount you borrow, you could be making a combined monthly payment of over $1,000. Depending on your entry-level salary and the average salary of your chosen profession, this could be a large chunk of your paycheck for an extended period of time.

The majority of the college graduates I spoke to list this as one of their biggest regrets. They didn't take the time to understand what types of loans they'd need before they were signing up. Nor did they research the corresponding salaries with the degrees with they were paying for. The result was a hefty monthly payment, working at a job they did not like, and being unable to build the type of life they wanted because of financial restraints. If they could do it again, they would have done more research.

According to data from EdVestinU, 46% of students regretted taking out their loans and 52% are struggling to pay them back. This is clearly an issue that needs to be addressed. A plan must be put in place to ensure you can pay back what you borrow. Furthermore, if you know exactly what you are going to school for and how much money you are actually borrowing, you will be less likely to regret that decision once you enter the workforce.

Again, I do not say this to scare you or deter you from taking out loans. I say this to underline the importance of being prepared for what is coming. These loans could result in additional financial stress. However, if you are building a career you enjoy and a life that you love, it may be worth it. You might be okay with making a few sacrifices the first few years after school. I also point this out to make sure that whatever college/trade school you choose is worth the money. We will talk about what makes a college worth the money in the next chapter, but remember that if you can't justify why College A is so much more expensive than College B, that could be a sign that you need rethink your choice.

6. Finish all your classes by studying hard and improving your GPA.

Your next goal aligns with your first goal. Finish strong. At some point, if you put in the hard work and did what needed to be done, you will be accepted into college/trade school or figure out what the next step in your life will be. It is tempting to treat this as the end of something. Yes, you are technically closing a chapter of your life. However, you have no time to waste. Senior year is not the end of high school but rather the beginning of the next big step in your life. Keep building on the habits you created. You are now the type of person who voluntarily studies harder for tests, puts more effort into projects, and seeks out new ways to become smarter and better. Trying your best in all aspects of life should become second nature to you. It is more important than ever that you are thinking differently about your education. You need to continue becoming a better student to be prepared for the demands of college classes.

7. Take over a fourth activity your parents are doing for you.

Lastly, you guessed it—take one last item off that list of things your parents are doing for you. I would suggest grocery shopping. I am not saying you should start paying for your own groceries. That might not make financial sense. But if you plan on going to college, you need to understand how to shop for groceries. You will have to know what to buy, what nutrition facts are essential, what prices are reasonable, and how to cook a few basic meals. By the end of your senior year of high school, you should feel comfortable doing your own grocery shopping and being able to cook a few simple meals for yourself. If you prepare now, this is another adult responsibility that will come naturally once you enter the real world.

The goals, facts, and advice I have laid out for each year won't cover every situation you will encounter. There will be times when you will be forced to make your own decisions. Remember, when in doubt, make the choice needed to build that life you started building mentally. Try your best to remember what opportunities high school can provide you and why you are there. Try not to fall into the trap your classmates will fall into when they do just enough to get by and put off making the tough calls. Lastly, don't get too stressed out about the small stuff that will pop up. The small stuff goes away. It's the big stuff that has the lasting impact.

For those of you who think I did not talk enough about the college selection process in this chapter, you are in luck!

CHAPTER 6:

TIME TO PICK A COLLEGE

As you may have noticed, this book is all about being prepared for not just the real world but also for all the important steps in between. One of those steps is choosing what you are going to do after high school. This chapter is going to focus primarily on college because it is what the majority of high school students tend to select. Despite this, I would like to state for the record that I do not think college is for everyone. If you think you fall into that category, I would advise you to keep reading the next few paragraphs.

College is not for everyone. I know I have said that a few times in this book, but it's worth repeating. The reason is that we live in a society that is increasingly pressuring us to go to college and continue our education. For some reason, we have demonized trade schools and almost removed them from the options list entirely. We've created a false narrative that people who don't go to college automatically earn less money and have less success in their career. The result of this is thousands of students, who should be learning a trade, are being shuffled into college classrooms and saddled with student loan debt so they can get a job they don't even want. The world needs plumbers, electricians, carpenters, trash collectors, and host of other employment focused on manual labor. Our society also needs to recognize that anyone can make a more-than-decent living at these jobs if they apply themselves.

If you have a plan, you can do just as well as anyone else who went to college.

Yes, there are studies out there that show that those with a college degree earn more than those who don't. However, that is not a reason to go to college. That is a reason to have a "college-alternative plan." The people mentioned in that study who are making less money are in that state because they didn't have a plan, not because they went to trade school and became a plumber or an electrician. Those people graduated from high school and took a random low-paying job. They did not realize how expensive life was going to be. If you have a plan, you can do just as well as anyone else who went to college.

In the last chapter, I asked you to take the Is College for Me? questionnaire. The purpose was for you to examine your feelings toward a few key elements of higher education. First, do you enjoy classroom learning on some level, or did your entire high school experience fail to inspire you in any way? Second, how does the idea of working in an office sound? If it sounds dull and boring, then maybe you shouldn't sign up for a major that is going to do nothing but place you into one of those jobs. Lastly, is college necessary for the jobs on your list and for the person you want to become? If you like fixing or building things or working with your hands, then maybe you should explore trade schools or alternative avenues of education.

It's important to understand that you can build any career you want, and there's no shame in choosing an alternative to college. You need to select the career path you want because you are going to be the one who has to live this life. There is no point in spending thousands of dollars on an education you will never use or is going to place you into a job that you hate. Even if you know already college is not for you, please keep reading. I promise to keep you in mind as we move through the next three college-centric chapters.

I want to point out right off the bat what this chapter is, and more importantly, what this chapter is *not*. This is not a chapter about the intricacies of the college application process. I will not be providing a checklist of every document you need to submit, nor will I be supplying you with a timeline of what is due when. It is also possible that your timeline might be different from what I'm saying in this book. You may do certain things in your senior year instead of your junior year or vice versa. Take control of the situation and understand what is going to work for you. Then, take this chapter as a guide to ensure you make the right choices based on what you want for your future.

This chapter talks about the factors that go into selecting the right college, factors that you may not think about. Like everything else, your college selection should prepare you for the real world and help you become your own person. Also, you need to research all that stuff on your own. Take ownership of the process.

Ideally, you want to start this process at the beginning of your junior year. Before you start you should have an idea of the career you want to pursue and what majors are aligned with those careers. You do not have to have all the answers, and you have the right to change your mind, but you should have some idea. If you are still struggling with this, then you may want to hold off until you have it figured out. Second, you should have an understanding of how much money for tuition you are receiving from your family. It's possible these two things might not be clear at the start of your junior year. If that is the case, you may want to hold off until you are ready. There is also the option of going to community college for a year while you figure these things out.

Community college is an option that is oftentimes overlooked. Your local community college is a low-cost option that will allow you to start your college education right away. If you are unsure of what major or career you would like, it may be cheaper and easier to take your basic courses at your local community school, then transfer somewhere else when you make your choice. In addition, it is possible that your desired career may only require 2 years of college education. Be sure to do the research so you do not end up wasting money at a 4-year school when a 2-year school will do the trick.

At this point in your life, a lot will be made about practicing for and taking the SATs. Again, I am not here to walk you through that process. There are more than enough resources online. I am here to point out that you need to take advantage of those resources. You should know whether the schools you are looking at require a minimum SAT score. The SATs are a big deal, but they are also just another step in a long line of steps that you need to prepare for on this journey.

The same thing goes for your college essay. Most, if not all, schools require you to pick a topic and write an essay about it. The goal of this exercise is for the school to learn more about you as a person and give you an opportunity to showcase your strengths and talents. Again, I am not an expert; I am advising you to seek out actual experts on this topic. This essay is a chance to showcase your passion and desire for building a life on your own terms. It is a perfect way to talk about the type of person you want to become and how that school is going to get you there. A lot of the research you did in high school can help you craft an essay that will stand out.

The reason I have dedicated an entire chapter to this step in your life is to underline to the importance of this choice. This is the first significant "domino choice" in your life. What I mean is that the college you choose will be the first in a long line of choices that will impact the rest of your life. Think about several lines of dominos lined up next to each other. Once you knock over the first one in the line, the rest will follow. This is similar to the series of choices you are about to begin. The major you choose to study will impact the college you go to. The college you choose will affect the amount of money you take out in loans, the people you meet, the opportunities you can take advantage of, and the classes you can take. When you graduate, your life will be impacted by those factors. If you took out a lot of money in student loans, you might have to move back home, and you might not be able to do the things you want to do right away. You will also be looking for a job. This is a process that will be made easier if you made the right connections in college (i.e., networked effectively) and if you took advantage of the opportunities the college provided. If you end up making large monthly loan payments, living at home, and working at a job you don't like, it will be challenging to build a life that you enjoy living. It is essential to see how your choices are connected and those "dominos" can keep falling for decades after college.

As you've read, this book's origin comes from the mistakes and missteps of students who have come before you. So many of the graduates I talked to told me about the mistakes they made and what they wish they had done differently when it came to college. I experienced this feeling, too. We will cover this topic more in the next chapter, The College Experience, but I do want to dive into specific regrets when it comes to researching and selecting a college.

Whatever the case was, their (in)action resulted in 4 years and thousands of dollars spent on an education that did not lead them to where they wanted to go.

The most common regret I hear from college graduates is that they did not spend enough time researching which college they wanted to attend. They did not understand the impact of the decision, but more importantly, some just figured most colleges were the same. We all know the Ivy Leagues are prestigious and unique, but to the untrained eye, what is the difference between Marymount University in Arlington, Virginia, and Marywood University in Scranton, Pennsylvania? Why should it matter if you go to Rutgers University or Ryder University? They are both located in New Jersey and seem to offer the same classes. This is another trap that many students have fallen into. They either did not do enough research or did not research the correct things. Whatever the case was, their (in)action resulted in 4 years and thousands of dollars spent on an education that did not lead them to where they wanted to go.

I also heard from a lot of people who said they wished they had spent more time researching different majors and courses of study before making a choice. This one hits home for me. If I had followed my advice own in high school, I would have been a journalism student. I enjoyed that class in high school, was a very good writer, enjoyed entertaining people, and did not care for sitting at a desk. Becoming a reporter or news producer would have been a favorable career path for me to take. Instead, I became distracted. I did not try very hard in high school. I did just enough to get by, and therefore my college choices were pretty limited. I became focused on simply getting into a college rather than what I was going to study. Once I got in, I majored in political science. Don't get me wrong—political science is a solid choice if you have an idea of what you want to do with that type of degree. For me, I was into politics at the time, so I thought I would choose this major and "figure it out later." Once I got into college, I started taking the necessary courses. At the end of my first semester, I met with my academic advisor. It was at this point when he notified me that a poly-sci degree, on its own, might not yield many options for me. Instead, I should pair it with another major such as education. So, I did, for the simple reason that I was told to— not a very good reason to change the direction of your education and future. That lasted less than a semester because I wasn't interested in it. Desperate to find a new career path, I chose public relations (PR). I can't exactly recall why I chose PR, but I suppose I thought it sounded like it was fun. While this choice has allowed me to build a career in marketing that I am proud of, it never really delivered the type of job and life that I was looking for. If I had gotten in touch with my inner passions and desires, I would have focused on a journalism career and followed a path toward a very different life.

I am trying to inspire you to make smart, well-informed choices to avoid paying for your mistakes when you are older.

The last regret many respondents had regarding college selection is not understanding the student loans they signed up for. I know we have hammered this point several times, so I won't dwell on it for too long here. Many high school students assume that all colleges are expensive, and therefore they have to take out student loans. They often merely apply for what they need and sign the agreement without understanding what they are signing up for. This is a dangerous practice in any situation. You should *always have a full understanding of what your agreements are* and the impact they might have on your current and future situation. Again, I am not trying to deter you from applying for student loans or steer you to choosing a college based solely on price. I am trying to inspire you to make smart, well-informed choices to avoid paying for your mistakes when you are older.

We are going to talk about what makes a college worth the money later in this chapter. For now, I have resupplied that pre-loan checklist I provided you with in the last chapter. Take another look, understand what you need to know, and be sure to ask these questions before you sign anything.

Pre-loan Checklist

1. What is the total amount of money I am borrowing?

2. What is the interest rate on this loan?

3. What is the total amount of money I will owe after college?

4. When will I have to start paying this loan back?

5. How much per month will I be required to pay?

6. If I only pay the minimum, how long will it take to pay back?

7. If I only pay the minimum, how much money in interest alone will I be paying?

8. Would this minimum amount be less if I chose a different school? How much less would it be?

9. Does this loan get deferred if I go to graduate school (if applicable)?

10. Do the terms of my first job affect the terms of my loan in any way?

11. Is it possible my loan could be forgiven or reduced if I enter into a specific job or industry?

It's time to undertake some personal discovery and figure out what excites you, what scares you, what are you passionate about, and what type of life will you be glad you lived when looking back on it 50 years from now.

Now that we have focused on others let's start to focus on you. Remember, you are the one who is going to have make all of this come together and work. You do not have to do it alone, but you will have to take ownership and commit to completing the challenging parts. The college selection process is a time to start discovering who you are as a person and what you want to accomplish with your career and your life. It's time to undertake some personal discovery and figure out what excites you, what scares you, what are you passionate about, and what type of life will you be glad you lived when looking back on it 50 years from now.

We have established how important this choice is and the effect it has on the various parts of your life. It is crucial that you make this choice personal. You have to understand what you are looking for in a college and what type of environment you are going to thrive in. Not everyone needs to go to a big-name school with a massive student body. Just like not everyone needs to go away to college. Also, not everyone needs to start their college education in a 4-year institution. This choice has to be personal. It is the only way to ensure that it is the best choice for you and your future.

Below is the Personal College Readiness Audit that I have created to help you in this process. This is designed to assist you in understanding your needs and what figuring out what type of college will work best for you. Like all the other audits, it is essential that you are open and honest.

Personal College Readiness Audit

1. Am I ready to hold myself responsible when it comes to attending classes, completing my schoolwork, and studying for my exams?

   a. If not, what do I need to do to fix this problem?

2. Am I able to complete basic adult tasks such as cooking, laundry, and grocery shopping?

3. Do I know what job, career, or general field of study I am working toward while in college?

4. Will I benefit from going away to college, or will I be better off living at home and being around family and friends?

5. Am I confident enough in my career choice to enter straight into a 4-year college, or would I benefit from first going to a community college until I solidify my choice and my plan?

This is an important exercise because it helps you get in touch with who you are a person, what you need to be successful, and what you need to work on as you enter into the next steps in your life. The questions in this audit are more profound and more complex than those in your previous audits, so let's break them down one by one.

1. Am I ready to hold myself responsible when it comes to attending classes, completing my schoolwork, and studying for my exams?

If you are currently the type of student who only studies when prompted or harassed by your parents, it is time to start taking responsibility for your studies. If you don't, it's likely that your grades will suffer, and you may never be able to recover. This particularly applies if you want to go away to college; you need to make sure you are ready for all the additional challenges that come with it. Whether you stay at home or go away for college, make sure you are ready to do the work expected of you.

2. Am I able to complete basic adult tasks such as cooking, laundry, and grocery shopping?

This falls in line with that parental tasks list I keep talking about, and it falls in line with the point I made above. Going away to college includes a lot more than partying and freedom. Again, to avoid issues in your freshman year and beyond, make sure you can answer yes to this question.

3. Do I know what job, career, or general field of study I am working toward while in college?

At this point, if you followed the steps I laid out throughout the high school years, you should be able to say yes to this question. If you are still unsure, that's okay. However, you have to consider what the best next move is for you. Does it make sense to take out loans to go to a 4-year school if you are unsure that you will be able to pursue the career of your choice? You may end up having to switch schools, which could mean more courses, which could mean more time (and more loans), which means more stress after graduation.

4. Will I benefit from going away to college, or will I be better off living at home and being around family and friends?

This is a personal question that has no wrong answer. A strong support system is key to anyone's success. Going away to college means leaving your family and friends, possibly far away, for the first time in your life. Do some soul-searching here. If you are the type of person who needs the support of your family close by, or someone who benefits from familiar surroundings, then your best next step is to pick a school to which you can commute from home. Plus, you will save money by not incurring moving expenses and/or having to reside at a dorm.

5. Am I confident enough in my career choice to enter straight into a 4-year college, or would I benefit from

first going to a community college until I solidify my choice and my plan?

This is similar to question #3, but it is worth repeating. You may follow all the steps and audits. You may do your research, create your plan, and connect with all the necessary people. After all that, you may still be unclear about what job or career you want to pursue. While it is frustrating, it is understandable. The key here is to not settle. Do not just pick something because you have to. Keep researching and asking questions. In the meantime, select a community college that will allow you to take your basic courses and save some money while you decide. You can always transfer to a bigger school in a year, once you have that career plan nailed down.

So, we have decided we are going to college: we are ready for college, we know what type of college is right for us, and what we can afford. Now comes the fun part: researching and visiting colleges. If you did everything I mentioned, you should have a slightly better idea of where to start your search. There are still a ton of college to choose from, but at least now, you won't waste time on any that are too expensive, too far away, or do not offer any majors that are going to help you become that person you have been building in your head.

I am not an expert on researching and selecting colleges. Therefore, I will not pretend to be one and tell you how to start creating your list of what colleges to visit. That is not the point of this book. The point is to get YOU to start thinking differently and get YOU to be excited enough to get started on your own. If you began that relationship with your high school guidance counselor, then that is a perfect place to start. He or she can help you begin to put together a list.

Another alternative is an app that was released in 2016 called myKlovr. This virtual-college-counseling platform accompanies current high school students bound for college, starting in the 9th grade, until the application submission. It uses data science and artificial intelligence to provide high schoolers and their parents with guidance on how to choose the right colleges and how to increase every student's chances of college admission. This is a platform and opportunity I would highly suggest any high school student check out. Between the app, your counselor, the answers to your audits, and the career research you have done, you should be able to compile a decent list of colleges to start visiting as well as put together your plan how to become a more desirable college candidate.

Many of these colleges may sound and look the same. It is easy to pick one simply because it has the major you want, a big-name sports team, or an impressive student center with a ping-pong table. In my case, I chose my college because it was the only one that accepted me. I slacked off in high school and no one wanted to take a chance on me. I made mistakes in high school, and then made another mistake by not exploring all my options when it came to college. When researching and visiting these schools, it is essential to ask the right questions. If you have come so far and worked so hard to get to this point, you owe it to yourself to do everything possible to make the right choice. Making the right choice here will help you with creating that life you have been curating.

Following is a list of questions that you should be asking yourself or your tour guide during or after every college campus visit.

How many majors can you choose from?

This may seem odd since we talked so much about doing the research needed to choose the right major. The reality is that after you enter into a major, you may discover it is not what you thought. You may also encounter someone or something that changes your mind regarding what career you want to pursue. If you are attending a college that only specializes in that major, you could find yourself in a tough situation. You may have to transfer to a different school. Transfer students often find that not all of the credits they earned can transfer over, thus they are forced to retake certain classes. It may benefit you to choose a school with a wide range of choices, just in case.

When do you have to declare your major?

This is important. Most colleges do not require you to declare a major at the start of freshman year. Depending on the school, you may not have to declare until the end of your freshman or sophomore year. While it is very beneficial to have a solid grasp on your career path before entering college, you may find yourself in a situation in which you have a few different majors to choose from. You may find yourself stuck between two similar types of careers. Rather than pick because you feel like you have to, take the time they are giving you to continue your research. Spend that time talking to professors from both majors and understand the coursework. Then, connect with alumni who are currently working in those fields. This way, when you have to make your choice, you will be making an informed decision and not just guessing.

How close is the campus to a major city?

You should not disqualify any school strictly because of its location. However, depending on your career choice, you may benefit from your school being close to a city that offers internships and job placement opportunities. If the school is close to a major city like New York, Chicago, or Philadelphia, it may have partnerships with various companies. The career center may have a reputation of being able to place students into internships and graduates into jobs. If your career path could benefit from such a situation, this needs to factor into your choice. It may also make the school worth the price if you find it is more expensive than your other options.

How successful are the alumni?

When it comes to judging someone's "success," it can be very subjective. If someone makes a lot of money, that person is seen as successful. Sometimes, success is gauged by someone's title or influence in the company or industry he or she works in. For the sake of this question, we are gauging the success of the school's alumni on whether they are working in their field of study, how long it took them to find their first position, and how much going to that school helped them obtain the career they currently have. You can ask your tour guide about this but be wary of the response. Your guide will tend to highlight that one tech grad who started in his own company or someone from the class of 1947 who went on to become a congressman. We are looking for a pattern of graduate success, not just a few impressive examples. The graduation rate is also fine, but look into what the alumni are up to. Log in to LinkedIn and look up working professionals from that college. Specifically, look at what they studied, whether they graduated from that school, how long it took to land that first job, and then what jobs they have had since graduation. This should give you a picture of what happens to graduates who attend that school.

Then, connect with a few of those alumni. Ask them direct questions about the school, such as what they liked and didn't like, did the college/university prepare them for the real world, what kind of resources and opportunities did they find valuable, and would they still go to that school if they had the chance to do it again. The answers could help bump a school to the top of your list or save you a lot of time and money by realizing the school is not for you.

In addition to these questions and like research, be aware of your surroundings when on a campus tour. If you are going to commit significant time and money to this school, you should know what you are signing up for. For example, if you are there on the weekend, what is campus life like? Is it a ghost town that seems as if all the students go home for the weekend? What seems to be the attitude of the students you see walking around? Do they seem happy and energetic, or sad and miserable? What are the buildings and classrooms like? Are they brand new with state-of-the-art technology, or are they old and run down? Does it seem like the college cares about taking care of the campus? It's important to learn as much as you can while on tour. Tour guides will make the school out to be the best one in the country because that is their job. It is your job to get the complete picture and figure out if it is the best one for you.

Lastly, you have to decide whether the college is worth the money. You do not have to choose the cheapest college, and you do not have to disqualify the most expensive one immediately. You need to look at how much each college on your list costs, figure out how much you can pay now, how much you will need to cover in loans, and what you learned about the school makes it worth it. If the most expensive college on your list has brand new buildings, happy and successful alumni, partnerships with major companies, and offers majors related to your desired career path, then it might be worth the money. On the other hand, if there is another college on your list that checks all or most of those boxes but is cheaper because it is lesser known, then it may be worth going there and saving your money.

Again, I can't answer these questions for you, but if you have started to think differently while reading this book, you should be able to answer them for yourself. You need to take everything you learned from your internal audits, campus tours, and college research and try and make a choice that is best for you.

You also need to take control of this process. Make a timeline of everything you need to do and when it is due. I cannot do this for you, because it will be unique to you and your needs. Only you truly know what you need to succeed.

Next stop: college.

CHAPTER 7:

THE COLLEGE EXPERIENCE

As you can clearly see, this chapter is going to cover college (or university). If you have chosen that college is not for you, I suggest still reading this chapter. It may change your mind, or it may solidify your choice even further. In this chapter, we are going to cover the first 3 years of your college education. The fourth year, your senior year, will be discussed in Chapter 8. Just like the chapter on high school, each year will have goals for you to work toward. However, this chapter is going to also dive into personal responsibility. We will focus on the choices you make outside the classroom, as well as the serious mistakes many students, including me, have made and repeated throughout the higher education years.

Before we get to any of that, I want to spend some time talking about something called "the college experience." The college experience is an idea that has been around for decades. Enhanced and supported by movies, television shows, and other pop culture, the idea is that the most important part of going to college is partying. Countless movies and shows depict characters as college students who do nothing but drink, party, and have a ton of fun. These college depictions often never show anyone going to class or studying, and if they do, it's brief and inaccurate. Somehow, going to college changed from preparing yourself for the rest of your life to spending 4 years partying every night and getting into trouble. Furthermore, it appears that we have been taught to treat going to class and studying as nothing more than an entry fee for this type of lifestyle.

While I had a blast in college, I never took my time there seriously enough to produce anything meaningful for the next steps in my life.

Don't get me wrong; I am not a saint. I went to college, and I partied. I went out and did some pretty stupid stuff. I never did anything serious, but I engaged in a pattern of behavior that was, at times, reckless and certainly affected my studying and my grades. I fell into the trap that society lays for us. I thought going to college was all about having fun and nothing else. I merely took my "do just enough to get by, and I'll figure it out later" attitude from high school and enhanced it. No, I never failed a class, and yes, I graduated on time, but the result of my college experience was a lackluster GPA and résumé. While I had a blast in college, I never took my time there seriously enough to produce anything meaningful for the next steps in my life.

As you may have guessed, I am not the only one who feels this way. In talking to college graduates along this journey, I've found that many of them have similar regrets. The answers vary, but the common theme is that they got swept up in what other people told them college was supposed to be like rather than defining it for themselves. This type of behavior, combined with the lack of caring and preparation in high school, left many of these students in a less-than-desirable state after graduation. They were entering the real world with nothing except stress and student loan debt.

By balancing the two, I would have had a college experience that would have been a ton of fun AND put me in a better position to succeed after graduation.

Let me be clear about this: I am not saying to not have fun in college. I would never say that, and I don't think you would listen to me if I did. What I am saying is this: create your own college experience. Figure out what you want it to be about and, more importantly, what you want the result to be. There is nothing wrong with going to parties and having fun as long as you don't lose sight of the overall goal. If I could go back in time, I would still do some of the things I did over again, but this time, I would also prioritize things like studying and being prepared for class. By balancing the two, I would have had a college experience that would have been a ton of fun AND put me in a better position to succeed after graduation.

There are a few points about college as a whole I would like to discuss before we dive into our year-by-year goals and strategies. The first is the importance of attending class. Up to this point, you have basically been forced to go to school. For the majority of your life, it was the law, and even if your state allows you to drop out at some point, chances are there is no way your parents were going to let you do that. If you missed class, your teacher made a note of it, and someone from your school most likely e-mailed or called your parents to inform them of this. You may have been living in a world where someone woke you up for school, made sure you got there on time, and did their best to sure you went to every class. Otherwise, you were going to be in a lot of trouble. Attending college classes is an entirely different experience.

First off, if you go away to school, you are 100% on your own to get yourself up for class. I would highly advise against having your parents call you to make sure you get up. This is a habit you need to get used to ASAP. Not only do you have to get yourself out of bed but now you also need to make your own breakfast and time how long it's going to take to get to class. If you attend a smaller college, you may able to walk. However, if you attend a larger college, you may need to take a bus or shuttle, which runs on a schedule. It's not going to wait for you like your mom did in the driveway during high school.

Going to afternoon classes can be a challenge as well. You will be living in a building filled with students who have a different schedule than you. Therefore, there will always be someone watching a movie or playing video games when it is time for you to go to class. No one is going to force you to leave. You need to be the one who understands that only by going to class will you be able to keep working toward that person, career, and life you are building in your head.

If you are staying home for college, it will be tempting to keep relying on your parents to wake you up and get you out the door. Again, it's time to start acting like an adult and taking responsibility for yourself and your actions. By starting now, you will avoid that culture shock that comes with being an adult. I did not stay home for college, so my knowledge here is limited. If this is your plan, be sure to talk to someone who also stayed home for college and try to pick up some useful tips.

Another aspect of attending class that is about to change is the enforcement of attendance. All high school teachers are required by law to take attendance. Therefore, it is their job to make sure you are in class. Also, as a high school student, you always have it in the back of your head that if you don't go to class, you are going to get in trouble with your parents. Therefore, you always have that underlying motivation that has nothing to do with actually wanting to learn what is being taught. Many college professors do not take attendance, and the ones that do certainly don't report it back to anyone in your family. If you miss a college class, they just maybe make a note of it and move on. If the only reason you ever went to class was to avoid getting in trouble, you just lost all your motivation. Some professors allow two to three absences before they start deducting from your grade. Once you cross that threshold, they begin deducting points from your final grade.

The last aspect of the importance of attending class involves actually being present while you are there. What I mean by this is that it is very easy to merely count showing up to class as a victory. It's easy to wake up late, skip showering, and sit in the back of the classroom. But if you're not actually engaging with what is being taught, what is the point? If you are not learning something and becoming a smarter person in the process, then why are you paying all that money? If you ignore what the instructor says, you might as well skip the class altogether. Either way, you are not learning the content and will be unprepared for your exams. This goes for your sleeping habits as well. If you are not getting enough sleep to be able to stay awake in class, then you are—again—wasting your time. You need to respect your studies enough to understand how much sleep you need to engage in the course, not just be half awake at the back of the classroom.

I was often guilty of this. I didn't sleep as much as I should have, and then I would sleep in and shuffle into class right as it began. I just kind of sat there in survival mode until it was over. Every time I treated a class this way, my grades would suffer. It also prevented me from developing any discipline or good work habits to translate into my first real-world job. My final GPA was one of my biggest regrets. If I'd had a goal to focus on and took responsibility for my choices, my grades would have reflected my real potential. I have no doubt this would have helped prevent a lot of stress when it came to looking for a job after graduation.

Stop doing things only because you think you have to. Start to do things because you understand the positive effect they can have on your future.

It comes down to this: if you don't take ownership over your life and choices, it can derail everything you want to accomplish. College is the time to start growing up and taking control of your life. This is why that list of things your parents are currently doing for you is so important. College is a big enough transition as it is, but it can be made impossible if you are also trying to learn how to do all of these things by yourself. That is why it is crucial to start to change your thinking in high school. Stop doing things only because you think you have to. Start to do things because you understand the positive effect they can have on your future.

College, especially for those who go away to attend it, will introduce you to all types of people. If you were like me, someone who grew up in a town where everyone was similar, this can be a bit of a transition for you. If you meet someone of a different background, I will encourage you to not only keep an open mind but to actively get to know them. It's easy to stick with people who look like you. You don't grow that way, though. You grow by meeting new people who can show you a different view of the world. It may be uncomfortable at first, but by meeting people who are different from you, you can improve your worldview. This will make you a smarter person and better prepared to work and communicate with the types of people you will meet out in the real world.

I also want to warn you of some of the other people you will meet in college. You will undoubtedly be meeting other students who are not preparing for their futures and are merely in college to party and have fun. These types of students tend to skip class, stay out all night, and get poor grades. They are not usually around very long and are kicked out before their sophomore year. Be careful about letting their bad habits affect you and your grades. There will always be people who will want you to skip class and hang out with them. Just like there will also be students who don't have class at that moment and are doing fun stuff like playing video games or watching movies.

It's easy to emulate what they are doing and get caught up in that "college experience" we spoke about earlier. Try to surround yourself with like-minded people—the type of people who will go to the library with you, motivate you to study, and will not encourage you to skip class for their benefit. Like-minded people are the types who can be invaluable to your current and future success and may even become lifelong friends.

Now we are going to break down college year by year. As I previously mentioned, senior year will be covered in its own chapter. This is important to read now, regardless of where you are in your journey. If you are in high school, you can begin to prepare yourself for college mentally. If you are already in college, it's a great way to see whether you are on track or in what areas you may have fallen short. And in the event that you are reading this during the summer before your freshman year of college, well, you are right where you need be! I would also suggest rereading this chapter at the beginning of each year, and more often if you feel like you have gotten off track (and hopefully not fully off the rails).

Freshman Year

Goals

1. Declare your major/determine when you have to declare.
2. Schedule classes on the basis of when you perform the best.
3. Meet with your academic advisor.
4. Create a schedule to include classes and study time.
5. Work toward a 3.0+ GPA.
6. Attend class at least 90% of the time.
7. Prepare for sophomore year.

Before we jump into the goals, I want to talk about your freshman year in general, especially for those of you going away to school. If you are staying home, it will be a little easier for you, because you will be going home every night to people you know and sleeping in your own bed. However, if you go away to school, your whole world changes very quickly. You are on your own, sleeping in a different bed, surrounded by a bunch of people you've never met before. You have to wake yourself up, do your own laundry, make sure you eat three meals a day, find your classes, get to know new people, and oh, by the way, take college-level courses and get good grades. It's overwhelming, and for some, college swallows them whole on Day 1.

Following is a list of a few basic tips for surviving your first month of being away for your freshman year. These should allow you to get your bearings and adjust to your new surroundings.

Be Careful Whom You Trust

Not only are you leaving your family and home behind, but you are leaving your close friends as well. These friendships were built over many years and probably provided a sense of comfort and security. Now that security blanket is gone, and you are being forced to make new friends.

It's easy to find someone you get along with, and you may want to become good friends with that person immediately. But all these new friends are just that—new. You don't know them yet. You may be yearning for the same type of bonds you had back home, but that took a long time to create. Some of your new friends may indeed become your best friends, but only time will tell. Until then, be careful whom you trust and what you say.

When in Doubt, Keep Your Mouth Shut

Your sense of humor may have worked back home with your group of pals who knew all about you. However, you are now with new people who are still forming their own opinions of you. Your hometown friends may know when you're kidding, but your new friends might not. Furthermore, you don't know the political or religious views of the new people you meet. What might be funny to you could be serious to them. It's better to be on the quiet side at first and begin to open up as time goes on. You would much rather have people say in a few years that they remember you were the quiet kid at first than to offend someone right off the bat and spend years trying to mend a relationship or fix your reputation.

Study in the Library

We are going to talk about the importance of studying outside the dorm, but I will touch on it here because it is crucial to creating this habit on Day 1. Living in a dorm means living with 20 or 30 people on your floor. There is always going to be people who are playing video games, watching a movie, or doing something more entertaining than the studying and homework you have to do. Do your work in the library from the start. Working in a space designed for schoolwork will ensure that you start college with good grades, and it puts you in a routine that will be easy to follow as your classes get harder. Again, there will be much more on this later, but I really want to hit home the dangers of skipping classes and studying in order to do the funner things happening in the dorms.

Set Two Alarms

This one falls in line with being independent and moving away from having your parents do everything for you. Odds are that you just spent the last 12 years being woken up by a parent or sibling for school. Being away from school means being away from the people who bugged you to get up. Furthermore, as was discussed earlier in this chapter, your college professor doesn't call home if you miss class. Instead, he or she deducts points from your grade and moves on. Set two alarms. One on your phone and one on an actual alarm clock across the room. This ensures that you can only snooze on one them. You may think this is trivial, but coming from someone who missed a quiz because he overslept, it's not.

Watch What You Eat

This one hits very close to home for me. Growing up, I never thought about what I was eating. I just ate whatever my parents gave me, and since it was usually healthy, I never had much of an issue. Then college came, and I ate whatever was in front of me. In my case, the dining hall that I walked into every day had French fries, ice cream, and cheeseburgers. Every. Day. As you may have guessed, I never gave a second thought to my eating habits and ate anything I wanted, every day, for 4 years. The result was I gained 85 pounds, which has taken years to finally work off. Now, this is an extreme example. Most people do not put on that type of weight. Most people put on 10-15 pounds. Some understand the importance of a balanced diet and going to the gym, and they don't put on anything. What I am saying is, make sure you are aware of what you are eating on a daily and weekly basis. Also, it may benefit you to work going to the gym three to four times a week into your routine.

I promise freshman year gets easier over time. You get used to the added responsibility and you meet new friends. In the beginning, you may often find yourself wanting to go back home, but that feeling will most likely dwindle over time. I remember when I first went away to school, my parents came to visit for the first time and I was crying to my dad about how homesick I was. That feeling disappeared pretty quickly after I ended up meeting some great friends whom I am still close with to this day.

If you follow these select but important tips, I promise you'll have won half the freshman-year battle. Now, on to the goals!

1. Declare your major/determine when you have to declare.

Before you chose your college, you should have either chosen your specific major or narrowed your choice of majors to a few, all lining up with the person you want to become and the life you want to live. If you know what major you want, be sure to fill out the necessary paperwork to declare before the school year starts. While most of your classes will be your basic classes, you may be able to take a few of your major courses in your first year. This is important for two reasons. First, it puts you on a track to graduate on time. Second, it gives you an idea of what the major is like, which can help solidify or question your choice, based on your experience in those classes.

If you are still undecided, this is even more important. Be sure to determine when the deadline is to declare. It could be as early as the end of your freshman year or as late as the end of your sophomore year. Regardless, find out the deadline and use that time to your benefit. Start with speaking to the professors and advisors in those majors. Ask questions that will give you a better idea of the coursework involved, and whether you should be declaring for that major before the deadline. Next, connect with alumni from your school who majored in those subjects. Ask them what they thought about the classes and what the job prospects were like after they graduated. Would they still declare the same major if they could do it all over again? If the alumni you are speaking to are currently working in the same field you want to be working in, ask them questions about their jobs. What is their workday like? What are the pros and cons of their career? The more information you can gather beforehand, the better choice you can make when it comes time to declare.

2. Schedule classes on the basis of when you perform the best.

Depending on your school, you may not be able to select the dates and times of your first-semester freshman-year classes. Even if you can, as a freshman, you usually have to select last, and therefore your options are limited. However, if you have some choices, choose the class times when you can perform at your best. For example, if you were never a morning person in high school and you can choose between an 8 am class, or a 10 am class, choose the 10am class. Likewise, if you are someone who gets tired at the end of the day, classes after 4 or 5 pm might not be for you. The college will offer you classes that start earlier than you are used to and also start later than you are used to. This could be used to your benefit if you're in touch with your needs and understand the environment you require to succeed. Regardless of what class times you choose and what class times you get stuck with, make a note of how the time of the class affected your performance. You have to select your classes every semester; understanding what times you do your best work can help you get the best possible grades.

3. Meet with your academic advisor.

Once you declare a major, you are assigned an academic advisor. This is the person who is supposed to guide you through college to ensure you are taking the right courses and are on the right track to graduate on time. Here is something to remember: unlike a high school teacher or guidance counselor, this advisor is not going to watch your every move. These advisors do not monitor your grades or make sure you go to class. If you skip meeting with them when you choose your classes, they are not going to look at your choices to ensure that selected the right courses. If you go to a college or university with a large student body, this advisor will have many students assigned to him or her. It is vital that you take the proactive approach to begin and maintain a relationship with this important person. Speak with your advisor often and ask any questions you have before making any important decisions.

Furthermore, unlike high school, you cannot just pop into

your advisor's office when you feel like. These professionals are often professors or other faculty members with busy schedules who are not always on campus. Be sure to make an appointment and show up with a list of questions and topics to discuss. You want to meet with your advisor at least three times during your freshman year. When you first arrive on campus, before you choose your second-semester classes, and at the end of the year when it is time to select your first-semester sophomore-year classes.

If you are starting college with your major as undecided because you are still researching your options, then you should attempt to meet with an advisor from each major you are considering. Again, be prepared with the questions you have about that specific major. The point of this meeting is to gather information for when it comes time to declare. It is possible that your college may also provide an advisor to undecided students. It is worth meeting with that person as well.

4. Create a schedule for your classes and study time.

One of the themes that you have probably noticed is that when you reach college, there are many things that you have been doing your whole life that have now dramatically changed. This fact alone is something most students were not prepared for. Attending school up until this point meant going to one place for a set amount of time. Your days began close to the same time every year, and they ended at almost the same time every year. College is a lot different.

College can create an illusion that you have a lot of newfound free time. During your senior year of high school, you probably went to school for 7 straight hours. It's likely your new schedule may only require 4-5 hours on certain days, and those classes maybe 2-3 hours apart. Being free from the classroom from 10am to 2pm on Tuesday is a brand-new experience. It appears as if you have 4 hours of newfound free time. I call this an illusion because you have to schedule your own time to do your homework and to study. You are no longer sitting at the kitchen table with your parents hovering over you, if that was your good fortune to experience that. It's super easy to head back to the dorm room, take a nap, or hang out with friends. It will also be very easy to keep doing that when it's time to go to your next class of the day.

Once you receive your class schedule, create your own calendar and punch in the dates, times, and locations of those classes. Then, schedule 3-5 hours of library time every week. You don't have to spend every free moment in the library. There will be plenty of time for video games and hanging out. This system will ensure that you are prioritizing your schoolwork. I suggest scheduling 1-2 hours of library time right after a class, especially if you can go somewhere and work in the same building that your class is in. Plus, you are already in the mindset to do work and won't be distracted by what is going on back at the dorm.

This point is important because you are laying the groundwork for a successful college career. Many of the graduates I spoke to regretted not making time for their studies. By starting these types of habits on Day 1, you are making it easier to maintain them all 4 years. As the years go on, your classes will get harder, and the number of hours in the library will increase. This goal is designed to help you prevent a very common mistake and tackle one of the most prevalent problems that new college students face.

5. Work toward a 3.0+ GPA.

It would be extremely beneficial if you graduated college with a 3.5 GPA or higher. That being said, I believe in setting realistic expectations for yourself. If you are going away to college, you are dealing with significant changes, possibly homesickness, and tougher courses then you are used to. If you are staying home for college, you are still dealing with tough courses, and most likely a job that takes up a significant amount of time. That is why I am challenging you to obtain and maintain a 3.0 GPA throughout your freshman year. If you are a high school student who always had a higher GPA, then, by all means, shoot higher. However, don't get down on yourself if your grades dip a bit in your first semester. You will understand the weight of these changes when they arrive, but for now, take my word for it.

There are also a few new reasons why it's important to keep an eye on your GPA. First off, no one else is doing it for you. As I said, it's your time to take control of your education. Your professors are not monitoring your grades, and neither is your academic advisor. They are too busy and are expecting you to be an adult and do this on your own.

Second, these grades do not get mailed home as your report cards did. Your parents cannot call the school and access your grades without your consent. For some, losing the motivation of getting yelled at for poor grades may be a big deal.

Lastly, most institutions have rules about maintaining a certain GPA to stay in your major, to stay in the dorms, or to remain in the school as a student. Remember, this is not a public secondary-ed school, where they are required to accept and keep you by law. Your college only wants the best, and if you are not living up to its standards, its standard-bearers will find someone who will. So, be sure you are calculating your GPA at the end of each semester. A 3.0 means a B—as long as you are getting Bs or better on most of your work, then you will know you are on the right track.

6. Attend class at least 90% of the time.

You may be surprised that I did not say 100% of the time. If you're a parent reading this, you may not be pleased that I did not say 100% of the time. Here is why I stopped at 90%. The advice I am giving and the plan I am laying out is designed to be reasonable and relatively easy to put into practice. It is highly unlikely in your freshman year that you will attend every class of every course, for both semesters. Why? Because life happens, and we are all human. No matter your best efforts, you will sleep through your alarm at least once. No matter how dedicated you are, you are going to give in to the human temptation of taking a break and skipping a class, especially your freshman year when you are taking basic courses. Any adults who tell you they never accidentally slept through an alarm or took a sick day when they weren't actually sick is probably lying.

Plan on going to every class. Create a series of habits and processes that are designed to ensure you attend all your classes. Most importantly, mark down when the tests are, so you do not miss those classes, AND you do not miss the review classes beforehand. Never miss two class sessions in a row, or on the same day. If you are struggling in a course, be sure to show up on time, every time. However, if you miss a class every once in a while and give in to the temptation of what's going on in the dorm, don't beat yourself up over it. You are human. But keep in mind that that attendance percentage number is going to go up in the coming years.

7. Prepare for sophomore year.

As I previously mentioned, you will choose your sophomore classes at the end of your freshman year. Be sure to consult with your advisor but also try and pick class times that fit you and your needs. Create a schedule that will not overwhelm you and that allows you ample time every day to focus on your schoolwork. The end of your freshman year usually means you get to choose your sophomore-year roommate. This is the person you will be living with, in close quarters, for several months. Choose someone you not only get along with but who also shares the same goals and ambitions as you, someone who will help motivate you to study and not try to talk you into skipping class and doing other things that distract from becoming that person you have created in your head.

When your freshman year ends, you should feel confident about your future. You should have achieved a high GPA, built up strong study and life habits, and declared your major. You should be going to class but also meeting new people and gaining knowledge to become a much more well-rounded person. Remember, it's all an adjustment, so let yourself slip up a couple of times without getting too down on yourself.

Sophomore Year

Goals

1. Calculate your GPA.
2. Meet with your academic advisor (mid-year).
3. Create your class and studying schedule.
4. Conduct first Internal College Audit.
5. Meet with a career center staff member.
6. Apply for your first summer internship.
7. Create a plan for your first internship.

1. Calculate your GPA.

Before your sophomore year begins, you should calculate your GPA and review all your grades from freshman year. This should not be new to you if you have been doing this since high school. We talked about the importance of your GPA already, so be sure it is at least a 3.0. Also, identify in what classes you got your best and worst grades. Why do you think that you received these grades? For your poor grade(s), perhaps it was the time of day you took the course, the fact that you sat next to a friend who distracted you, or maybe it just did not interest you. Understanding where you fell short will help you immensely in moving forward. This way you can avoid falling into the same traps over and over again.

2. Meet with your academic advisor (mid-year).

As we discussed, you will need to meet with your advisor at the end of your freshman year when it comes to explaining what classes to take for your sophomore year. Be sure to meet again before your second semester. It may be tempting to choose what you think you need or to choose the easier, later classes, but this is how former students have gotten into trouble. They took classes without consulting anyone and then found out later on that they took the wrong classes and could not graduate on time. Also, taking unnecessary classes means spending more money to take the right ones. Only you are responsible for ensuring you take the right courses each semester.

3. Create your class and studying schedule.

A new set of classes means a new schedule to create. How did your freshman studying schedule work out? How dedicated were you to it, and did it positively or negatively affect your grades? Take some time to take what you learned and apply it to this schedule you are creating now. This is the year you will start taking courses that are related to your major. It is imperative that you not only get good grades but that you also take the time to actually learn everything that is being taught. Be sure to add additional library and studying time around those courses. When the semester begins, examine the syllabuses given to you by your professors. Determine whether you are setting aside enough time based on when you have your biggest tests and when projects and papers are due. This is an exercise you are going to repeat before every semester.

4. Conduct first Internal College Audit.

This brings us to another internal audit. These audits are crucial because they allow us to check in with ourselves. Audits afford us the opportunity to have an honest conversation about how we are feeling and whether we are doing what needs to be done.

This particular audit is crucial because it can change the course of your college education, depending on what you answer. So be honest and use these answers when planning the upcoming year.

Internal College Audit

1. What was the most challenging aspect of starting college?
    a. How did you overcome it?
2. What class did you get your best grade in and why?
    a. How can you apply this to your other classes?
3. What class did you get your worst grade in and why?
    a. How can you fix this so it does not happen again?
4. Were you consistent about how much time you spent studying each week?
    a. If not, what will you do to improve?
5. Did activities such as partying, video games, and going out affect your grades?
    a. If yes, what can you do to ensure this does not happen again?
6. Did you take advantage of the opportunities your school gave you to learn more about your major or the real world in general?
7. What did you do to learn about your chosen field of study?
8. What will you do this year to learn more about the types of jobs associated with your field of study and what those jobs entail?
9. Are you still committed to becoming the same type of person and pursuing the same type of job that you were in beginning of your freshman year?

Take the time to answer these questions in a way that will provide you with the information you need to build upon your freshman year. These answers will show you what worked and should be repeated and what didn't work and needs to be fixed. It's also important to be sure you are still working toward the same goals.

5. Meet with a career center staff member.

One of the most significant opportunities a college can offer you is the career center. This is a department solely dedicated to the success of your career after you graduate. The career center is filled with people who can help you create your résumé, find internships, make valuable connections, and ultimately help with your job search. This book emphasizes relationships, and this is one of the most important ones you can make.

In the first month of your sophomore year, schedule a meeting with a member of the career center staff. The point of this meeting is to introduce yourself and talk about your major, as well as the jobs and companies you are interested in. This allows the career center to start looking out for you when it comes to internship opportunities. It also begins the process of creating your résumé and cover letter. This is the first significant step in preparing yourself for the real world. It is a step that most college graduates don't take until right before senior year. At that point, the impact a career center can have is limited because there isn't enough time to make up for all the time that was lost.

6. Apply for your first summer internship.

Most majors will only require one or two internships. Traditionally, college students attend those internships toward the end of their college careers. The issue with this tradition is that it creates a society of students who are graduating into fields without knowing what they are getting themselves into. They do not have the internship experience necessary to have a firm grasp on the day-to-day life that goes along with the jobs they are applying to.

I talk a lot about opportunities, and this is a big one. Internships allow you to get a clear picture of what a specific job or career is like. You get the chance to see what the day-to-day routine like is for someone in that position, as well as the everyday operations of the company as a whole. It also lets you meet people who are currently doing the jobs you may want to do someday. You can ask them questions about their positions and gain insight on what they do on a daily basis. These are connections that can prove valuable after graduation when you are applying for jobs. When you meet with the career center, express your interest for a summer internship in your area, and then follow up throughout the year to ensure you obtain one.

7. Create a plan for your first internship.

Just like everything else when it comes to your education and future, it is not enough to simply show up. At the time of writing this, the majority of internships are unpaid. That could change someday, but that is the way it is in 2019. I understand that working for free does not sound like a lot of fun, and it may appear unfair. Again, it is about thinking differently about the opportunities in front of you. It is also important to understand that there are types of "payment" that do not include money. If you create and execute a plan for your internship, you will be compensated in knowledge, experiences, and connections that can help you in a big way just a few years down the road.

Decide on what three things you want to learn during your internship. What are three pieces of information or skills that can help you in pursuing your career? Then, commit to learning three new things. Commit to being open-minded and asking questions so that you can learn three new ideas, skills, or pieces of knowledge that will make you a more knowledgeable person and a better student and employee.

Lastly, introduce yourself to as many people as you can and ask a lot of questions. Remember, if you are not being paid, you are being compensated in connections and knowledge. Start with the people in your department. Learn as much as you can about the different jobs associated with your course of study. This type of fact-finding can help you prepare for your first job out of graduation. It is also a great way to confirm you are on the right track.

It is possible that your internship may also shine a light on some things about your future career that you may not like. It's important to take each issue and examine it carefully. For example, you may find that most of the people you met didn't like their jobs. This could be a red flag, or it could be the fault of poor company culture. If someone is showing signs of disliking their job, be sure to ask what it is they don't like. If you build a strong enough relationship, you may even feel comfortable enough to ask this person if they would choose this career over again if they had the choice.

If, after your first internship, you feel very strongly that this type of career is not for you, it might be worth exploring changing your major. Before you do that, I would highly suggest you do two things. First, meet with your academic advisor. Explain the situation and explain why you are thinking of changing. Chances are, they have had these types of issues with past students and might be able to ease some of your concerns. Second, be sure to connect with similar professionals from other companies and ask them about their day-to-day activities. If everyone gives you the same answers, that field might not be for you. This is a choice you have to make on your own, but if, after getting a taste of your career, you're having second thoughts, take control of the situation and seek out the advice needed to make the best choice for your future.

Junior Year

Goals

1. Meet with your academic advisor/ensure you're on track to graduate on time.
2. Calculate your GPA.
3. Conduct second Internal College Audit.
4. Attend Class 98% of the time.
5. Apply for your second internship (during school year).
6. Apply for second summer internship.
7. Connect with five working professionals.
8. Work with career center to create résumé and cover letter.

By junior year, you should have a few things completely nailed down. You should feel comfortable with your choice of major and have a general understanding of the types of jobs you will be applying to. Your study habits should be strong, and you should be creating a class and study calendar every semester and sticking to it. This is the year to really start preparing for the real world. A lot of your goals this year are going to be focused on preparing you for life after college. The reason we are starting now, and not in senior year, is to get a leg up on the competition. This whole book is about doing things differently, acting with urgency, and preparing before it's necessary.

1. Meet with your academic advisor/ensure you're on track to graduate on time.

Meeting with your academic advisor at the end of every semester should be routine at this point. At the start of junior year, make an appointment to talk about graduation. Review the classes you have taken, your overall GPA, your major GPA, and the courses you still need to take. This is a checkpoint on the road to graduation. You want to confirm you are on track to graduate on time. You also want to verify that you have the GPA needed to earn that major. Remember, some colleges have one minimum GPA to remain a student and different minimum GPAs for the various majors.

If you followed the steps, did your yearly calculations, and followed your plans, then this should be an easy meeting. However, it's worth the 30 minutes to confirm you are on the right track. On the off chance you are missing a course, you can always take an extra class during the semester, during winter break, or during the summer.

2. Calculate your GPA.

Calculating your GPA every year should be a default habit at this point in your journey. At the bare minimum, you should be above a 3.0. Ideally, you want to be working toward a 3.5–4.0. A higher GPA can help you stand out when you are applying to entry-level jobs. With a limited work history and a résumé that can look similar to everyone else's, you need something that will attract the attention of the hiring manager who is reading it. Some students may not even put their GPA on their résumé because they are embarrassed by it. This will only make you look better by comparison.

If you are struggling to get to that 3.5+ plateau, perform an analysis on why you are struggling. Are you studying as often and as long as possible? Are you letting noneducational distractions get in the way of studying the proper amount? Are you having trouble retaining the knowledge you are being taught? Try to pinpoint the issue and create a plan to solve it.

3. Conduct second Internal College Audit.

At this point, you're halfway done with college. In 2 short years, you will be out in the real world. Two years may seem like a lot of time, but I want you to think how quickly the last 6 years just flew by. This next audit is critical because if you discover any issues, you are running out of time to fix them. Below is the same audit as before, with a few tweaks of course.

Internal College Audit

1. What is the most challenging thing about being a college student?

      a. How will you overcome it in your final 2 years?

2. What class did you get your best grade in and why?

      a. How can you apply this to your other classes?

3. What class did you get your worst grade in and why?

      a. How can you fix this so it does not happen again?

4. Were you consistent about how much time you spent studying each week?

      a. If not, what will you do to improve?

5. Did activities such as partying, video games, and going out affect your grades?

      a. If yes, what can you do to ensure this does not happen again?

6. Did you take advantage of the opportunities your school gave you to learn more about your major or the real world in general?

7. What did you learn during your summer internship that will prepare you for your career?

8. What will you do this year to learn more about the types of jobs associated with your field of study and what those jobs entail?

9. Are you still committed to becoming the same type of person and pursuing the same type of job that you were in beginning of your freshman year?

4. Attend Class 98% of the time.

It's important to understand the seriousness of going to class from here on out. The first 2 years, I gave you a break.

You were in a new environment, on your own, with a lot of temptation around you. At this point, you should be fully immersed in your college environment and used to prioritizing your future over any temporary distractions you may come across. All your classes from here on are tied to your major, which means they are going to help shape the type of person you want to become. It's important to soak up as much of this knowledge as you can. Also, missing class can affect your grade, which affects your GPA goal.

Another reason that going to class every day is so important is because it is a habit you need to start building. A job in the real world requires you to show up and perform every day. By attending and participating in every class, every day, you are preparing your mind for the routines of the real world. If you do this for the next 2 years, you will be better prepared for this aspect of working full time, which will lead to less stress and more fulfillment in your career.

5. Apply for your second internship (during school year).

We spoke earlier about the importance of internships. I suggested taking your first one during the summer because it gives you more time to get adjusted to a new situation. It may be the first time you are working in an office or longer hours, and it's easier to adapt to a new environment if it is one of the only things on your plate. It may be tempting to hold off jumping into another internship, but I strongly disagree. One of the most significant adjustments I had to make when I got my first office job was getting used to sitting in one place, all day. The other significant change was having less free time.

This is something that you need to prepare for so it doesn't smack you in the face when you graduate.

Applying for an internship during your second semester of junior year is a great way to prepare for what it will be like working in the real world. It will challenge you to balance your schoolwork, studying, and working a real job. You will have to be organized, plan out your time, and get adjusted to working more and hanging out less. I know this might not sound like fun, but it's a lot easier to start getting used to this lifestyle now because it is coming for you regardless of whether you prepare for it. Talk to your career center staff at the start of the year to figure out when the best time is to apply for internships next semester.

As for what type of internship you should apply to, I would try to make it as different as possible from your previous summer internship. If your previous internship was a big corporation, try finding a small business or nonprofit. Choose a different industry. Make sure that this position provides brand new experiences, knowledge, and skills. It is the only way to learn what you like, what you don't like, and what types of environments are going to keep pushing you forward into becoming that person you want to be.

6. Apply for a second summer internship.

Keep the internship train rolling! This is the time to explore and research your future paths. Meet as many people as you can and ask as many questions as possible. Also, remember to connect with these professionals on LinkedIn so you can call on them when you are searching for a job. As I said before, try to find an internship that will open you up to new experiences.

Also, it might be worth trying to intern at a company near your hometown. It is possible you may be able to return the following summer after graduation and apply for a job there. Meet with the career center at the start of the second semester of your junior year to figure out when to start applying for summer internships.

One last important thing about internships before we move on: at every internship, you should be trying to build a lasting professional relationship with at least one person there. You want to be able to leave an internship with at least one reference to use when applying for future jobs. A "reference" in this context is someone who will vouch for you being a good employee. When it comes time to apply for jobs after graduation, being able to hand over a list of five references, all ready to talk about how awesome you are, is going to be a big help. When you find that person, make it a point to stay in consistent contact throughout the year.

7. Connect with five working professionals.

I want to talk more about the importance of making professional contacts before you graduate. This has come up in several points in our conversation and journey, but let's tackle this head on. There's an old saying, "It's not what you know, it's who you know." I don't agree entirely with this because I know that if you do not have the skill set to perform at your job, you will be replaced, regardless of who you know at the company. I believe it's a little bit of both.

There are two main reasons for making reliable connections with at least five professionals currently working in the real world—first, the ability to ask questions of those who have come before you. I have stressed the importance of creating a LinkedIn account for this very reason. Whatever job or career you are pursuing, it is certain that some people are already in that position. Therefore, they have the answers to almost all your questions. By connecting with them, you can understand what that career is like and how to achieve it. It will also give you additional information to either confirm you are pursuing the right career or that you may need to make adjustments. These contacts can paint the picture of what your career and future will be like, and that's the perfect way to be prepared for the next step in your life.

The second reason is the ability to have someone to reach out to. After graduation, you will be among thousands of others looking for a job. Even after you land that first job, the day will come where you will be ready to move onto a better position. If you have spent the previous few years having meaningful conversations with working professionals, you will be able to call on them when you begin your job search. They may be able to recommend you for a position in their company or point you in the direction of another company they think you would like. They also can put you in touch with their contacts and recruiters in their field. Lastly, they can give advice on what to include on your résumé, how to answer certain interview questions, and what positions to look out for. I cannot stress enough the importance of building your own network while you are still in college.

8. Work with career center to create your resume and cover letter.

At this point, you should have a solid relationship with the staff at the career center. You have worked together to apply for internships and ensure that you are doing what needs to be done to prepare for a long and successful career. Also, at this point, you probably already have a résumé created for the internships you applied to. Regardless, this is the time to sit down with someone and build your first real résumé and cover letter. You want to be sure you have a résumé that is clean and tells a story. The story you are describing is one of a college graduate who works hard, has a vision, has obtained valuable skills, and will be an asset for any company.

The core of your résumé will be your internships, so you want to make sure you are highlighting all the important tasks you completed and skills you learned. Work with the staff to figure out how to write bullet points that will stand out from other résumés and really hammer home the points we listed previously. It is also essential to do your own research here and ensure your résumé speaks to your specific industry. What will the types of companies you will be applying to be looking for? What particular things do you need to call out? Is it suggested that you list the relevant classes you took? The answers can be found by talking to those working professionals we just spoke about.

The second item to create is your cover letter. A cover letter is a short introduction for someone to get to know you before reading your résumé. This is your avenue to talk about your passion for that field and how this field will help you become the person you want to be and have the life you want to live. Again, do your research and figure out what the hiring managers in your field are looking for. Understand that your first draft is merely a template. You will adjust the cover letter depending on where you are applying. For example, you will always want to list the specific position and why you are applying. Some of your past internships and jobs will be more relevant than the rest, so you will want to create a section that highlights that relevant experience. Between the career center staff and your network, you will be able to create a thoughtful cover letter that can be used as another way to stand out from the crowd.

By the time you end your junior year, you should feel confident about entering the real world. You are not there quite yet, but you have done everything you needed to do to be prepared. You have completed two internships and are getting ready to start your third. You are having regular check-ins with your academic advisor to confirm you are on track to graduate. You are having routine meetings with the career center to ensure you are ready to tell your story and pitch yourself to any company out there. You have built a network that is helping you plan for your future and giving you a solid idea of what post-college life will be like. You are almost ready to go. However, before we get there, we must enter into senior year of college. Let's do it!

CHAPTER 8:
OH MY, I'M ABOUT TO GRADUATE!

I named this chapter as such for a specific reason. College graduation will come faster than you think. One minute, you are moving into your freshman dorm and the next you are crossing the stage, getting your diploma. Listen to me and every single college graduate I have ever spoken to who agrees with me: college will go faster than you could possibly imagine.

This is yet another pain point that many students who came before you were not prepared for. Graduation from college means so many things, that it really does need its own chapter. It signals the end of a significant part of your life. It also kicks off arguably the most important part of your life. Your responsibilities go up, and your free time goes down. A lot will change as soon as you cross that stage. The world that awaits you is going to expect a lot more than it ever did before.

This chapter is going to cover all of it. We will include your senior year goals and how to make the most out of it, just like we have done every year up until this point. We are also going to cover what else is coming in your life and how to be ready for that as well. No matter where you are in your educational journey, this chapter is written to cap off your ride into the real world.

Oh My, I'm About to Graduate!

For most, this is too late, and they end up getting thrown into a world they know nothing about, taking a job they don't want, and living a life they never intended on living.

None of what I am going to say is going to be useful if you did not follow the goals, audits, and advice laid out in the last seven chapters. I mention this because some college students wait until this point in their lives to start thinking about their futures. When the respondents to my survey questions talked about putting off tough choices, not taking advantage of resources, and not putting in maximum effort, this is what they mean: waiting until the beginning or end of senior year to start thinking about life after college. For most, this is too late, and they end up getting thrown into a world they know nothing about, taking a job they don't want, and living a life they never intended on living.

As we have covered in the previous seven chapters, this thing we call "the real world" is pretty complicated. Not only are you working for most of your week but you are taking care of every aspect of your life, and someday you may be responsible for taking care of other people as well. If you didn't prepare up into this point, then there is no possible way to be ready for what's coming next. If you didn't research your loans, then you will be shocked when you see how much per month you need to pay back. If you didn't do any internships or prepare your résumé, then it is going to be incredibly difficult to find a job to help pay back those loans or move out of your parents' house. This moment will come very fast. This moment will also be overwhelming and impossible to navigate if you put off everything we have talked about up until now.

When you enter your senior year, you should already know what awaits you after college. You have now completed three internships, made several contacts, and compiled a list of reliable references. You have created a network for yourself, a group of working professionals who can answer your questions, give you advice, and help you achieve the career goals you have set for yourself.

You should also have a solid understanding of what your career path looks like, what types of jobs to apply to, and what those jobs are going to entail. The research you have done and contacts you have made should have answered most of your questions and given you enough information needed to avoid any big surprises or major issues.

Lastly, you should have no problem prioritizing your studying and getting good grades. You have confirmed you will graduate on time and have a full understanding of what you need to finish up in your last year. Following is a list of goals. They are just as important as any other year, but since many are repeats, I will not spend the time repeating what you should already know and be doing.

Senior Year

Goals

1. Perform your last Internal College Audit.
2. Meet with your academic advisor one last time.
3. Apply and plan for your senior-year internship.
4. Create your class and studying schedule.

5. Attend class 99% of the time.

6. Obtain a 3.5+ GPA.

7. Finalize your résumé, cover letter, and references.

8. Reach out to your network before graduation.

9. Begin you job search.

1. Perform your last Internal College Audit.

This is your last Internal Educational Audit, and it is focused on finishing strong and being prepared for what's next. Following is the list of questions. You know the drill. Open and honest is the only way to go. As always, these answers are useless if you do not take them and create a plan around them. This audit will look different than the previous two because you need to have an eye on the future. It will also look different because, at this point, you should know the answers to the most basic questions I have asked previously. Lastly, by the time your senior year hits, there is only so much improvement you can do. You should be in a good place and ready to move onto the next phase of your life.

Internal College Audit

1. Can you honestly say that your GPA is a result of you working as hard as possible?

    a. If not, what can you do this last year to improve it?

2. Were you consistent about how much time you spent studying each week?

    a. If not, what will you do to improve?

3. Did activities such as partying, video games, and going out affect your grades?

    a. If yes, what can you do to ensure this does not

happen again?

4. Did you take advantage of the opportunities your school gave you to learn more about your major or the real world in general?

5. What did you learn during your internships that will prepare you for your career?

6. What will you do this year to learn more about the types of jobs associated with your field of study and what those jobs entail?

7. Are you still committed to becoming the same type of person and pursuing the same type of job that you were in beginning of your freshman year?

2. Meet with your academic advisor one last time.

At this point, your relationship with your academic advisor is strong. You meet two to three times a year about your courses and your progress. You already met last year about your first-semester senior-year classes and to ensure you are on track to graduate on time. All that is left is one last meeting before your last semester—one last check that you fulfilled all your requirements to graduate on time.

If, during your research and networking, you have discovered that you would benefit from obtaining your master's degree, you may want to speak with your advisor about this earlier in the year. Whether you should pursue your master's depends on your major and the career you are seeking. If you have found that the majority of the people in your field have their master's, then that's something you will most likely have to pursue. On the other hand, if the contacts you've made went straight into the workforce and never looked back, then you might be okay with just your bachelor's.

Remember, a master's degree may mean more student loans and more debt for your future. That does not mean do not do it, it just means making your decision on the basis of research and what is going to help you achieve the life you are trying to build for yourself.

3. Apply and plan for your senior year internship.

As we spoke about, some majors only require one internship to graduate. For many, their senior year internship is the only one they will have. For you, this will be your fourth internship. At this point, you have ideally interned at three different companies, of varying sizes and environments. This last internship should be at a company you believe you would want to work for. It should be a challenging experience in which you perform real-world tasks and learn appreciable skills. When interviewing for this internship, talk about your past internships and your desire to do more than basic, entry-level tasks. Apply for the one that is going to give you something to talk about on your interviews when you start applying for jobs.

This internship should be the crown jewel of your résumé. It should be the one that sits atop the list and begins to tell the story of who you are and the type of value you can bring to a company. It should be a story that will continue to be told through your other internships. Challenge yourself to learn as much as you can. Also, ask questions about what kind of skills you need to obtain the entry-level jobs at that company. Sit down with someone from the human resources department and gain a solid understanding of what types of questions you might get asked in an interview and how to answer them properly. Use this time to prepare for the series of interviews you are about to embark on.

4. Create your class and studying schedule.

You know what you need to do here. This should come easy and should be the most effective schedule you have created because you are learning from all past mistakes and shortcomings. You know when you need to study and for how long. Don't slack off now; finish strong by creating a schedule that is going to produce your best grades yet. You may be tempted to shorten your studying time because college is coming to an end and you want to cram in as much fun as possible. Like I said, of course, you should have fun, but remember that when the fun is over, the rest of your life is still going to be waiting there for you. Be sure to enjoy these last few months with your friends, but do not forget about what you have been building toward this entire time.

5. Attend class 99% of the time.

Unless you are sick, you are going to class. Full disclosure: I did not follow this rule, and it hurt me. I started senior year with the mentality that my "fun time" was running out and that I should do whatever I wanted while I was still in college. I went to class most of the time, and I passed everything, but my discipline and focus were severely lacking. I missed a few key lessons, which hurt my ability to do well on my tests, which in turn ended up affecting my grades. I also was not building up those habits of going to class and participating. I needed those habits when I entered into the real world, and when they were not there, I suffered. Like we mentioned in the previous section, the temptation will be strong to skip out on your classes because you feel your time is running out. Coming from someone who did this and paid the price, I would highly suggest you remember why you started this journey in the first place. Remembering what you are working toward will provide you with the motivation you need to finish strong.

6. Obtain a 3.5+ GPA.

At first, we worked toward a 3.0. We let ourselves slip up a little bit and get adjusted to our new surroundings. If you have calculated your GPA every year, made your study schedules, stuck to them AND used the answers to your audits to create new habits, then a 3.5 or better GPA is attainable. This goal is another way to motivate yourself to that finish line. You know what kind of career you want, and after all your networking and interning, you should be pretty excited about getting started. So, if you want that job, and if you are excited about the type of life you are building for yourself, then you should be pushing yourself for the 3.5 GPA to put on your résumé. That GPA can be the driving force behind you getting your foot in the door at your first job and starting your journey toward becoming that person you just spent over 7 years of building in your head.

7. Finalize your résumé, cover letter, and references.

The second semester of your senior year is the time to get all of this in order. Do not wait until after graduation because then you will be home and on your own. You will also be at the same starting point as thousands of other college graduates.

This is the time to schedule a meeting with your career center contact and review all three of these documents.

Your résumé should be ready to tell the full story of what kind of value you are going to bring to a company. It should list every internship you had, all clubs you were a part of, and any awards that you won. Being aware that you are going to need these things to build your résumé will give you the motivation you need to go out and do them. Your résumé should also include the 3.5 GPA we just spoke about.

Your bullet points should be creative, and they should describe all the tasks you have completed—the projects you have worked on and the skills you have obtained. It should also include the information that hiring managers in your field are looking for. Be sure to talk with your career center about adding the right key words and the different types of résumé scanning systems that companies are currently using.

Your cover letter should be all set to showcase your passion and outline what you have been working toward. Do not be afraid to be open, honest, and genuine when talking about your desire to become the person and live the life you have been building in your head. This cover letter should also be customized for wherever you are applying. Some of it will remain the same, but be sure to point out the skills you have that relate directly to the position you are applying for. Mention the position by name and at least one reason why you are applying to that specific company. Hiring managers read hundreds of "one size fits all" cover letters, and you want to stand out from that crowd. A personalized cover letter will show them how serious you are about working for and contributing to their company.

8. Reach out to your network before graduation.

The last 3 years have been spent building a network. First, we used LinkedIn, our advisor, and our career center to find alumni and working professionals who were currently in the careers we were looking at. Then, we made it a point to form relationships at our internships with people who can vouch for our value. You have been keeping in contact with these people, asking them questions, and building useful relationships for your future. The second semester of your senior year is the time to start reaching out to that network about possible job opportunities.

First, make sure everyone in your network has your latest résumé and cover letter. Do not assume they kept the last version you sent them. Also, your network can expand beyond the people I just mentioned. Be proactive and send your résumé and cover letter to anyone in your family or friends who might be able to help get you an interview. Even if they cannot help you now, you never know what relevant positions can open up in the future. One of the best marketing jobs I ever had came after my second time interviewing with that company. The first time I interviewed and did not get the position. However, when a similar position opened up again, the hiring manager remembered me, and I ended up getting that job.

You want to start now to get a jump on your competition. I cannot stress enough how many recent college graduates will be out there. You will have similar degrees from similar schools, and it will be a challenge to differentiate yourself from this pack. The people in your network will see a lot of résumés around graduation time, and you do not want to get lost in that shuffle. You want to make sure that you are one of the first people making contact and getting their help.

9. Begin your job search.

As I mentioned before, you might choose to go straight into your master's. I cannot tell you if that is a good idea or a bad idea because I am not you. However, you should not be looking to me for that type of advice. Why? Because you should have done the necessary research and outreach and gathered the required information to make such an important choice. If you have chosen to pursue your master's, I would highly advise you sit down with someone who has pursued the same degree and get an idea of what the course load is like, including how many hours you might be able to work in a supplemental job.

For those stopping at a bachelor's, applying for jobs before graduation may seem a bit out of order. Hear me out on this, though. Looking for full-time employment is another huge change that you need to prepare yourself for. We will dive into that in the next chapter. That being said, we have stressed the importance of being ahead of the curve and the competition, and this is no different. Once your résumé and cover letter are complete, your references are confirmed, and your network has been contacted, you should begin the process of looking for jobs. I would suggest starting in late April or early May. Again, we are going deeper into this topic in a minute, but if you are planning out your senior year, plan to spend some time before graduation to begin this process.

I have met people who took a year off after graduation to travel. Whether this is a good or bad idea is not for me to say, but I will say this: determine what that time off is going to do to your career. First off, how are you financing this venture?

You won't be working, and you will be spending money on a daily basis while you travel. If you have student loans coming due, does it make sense to put off making money and put yourself further into debt? Second, are you working in an industry that will look down on someone who has not been "in the game" for an extended amount of time? These are some important factors to consider. That being said, if you can afford it, and feel confident that it will not hurt your job prospects, then it might be the right move for you.

It is my hope that you truly understand how quickly this moment will arrive. I was entirely unprepared for the day I crossed that stage.

Graduation is an emotional time. If you went away to school, you have spent 4 years growing up with a group of people who have become your close friends. You have been through ups and downs, good times and bad times. Depending on where you are in the country, these friends who you have seen every day may be going back to a home that is a long way from where you live. It's okay to have mixed emotions about graduating. It's also okay to want to take some time away from studying to spend with these people before it is all over. It's about balancing the two to ensure you create the college experience you want AND build the life you want to live at the same time.

It is my hope that you truly understand how quickly this moment will arrive. I was entirely unprepared for the day I crossed that stage. I spent 8 years saying I would figure it out later. Then, later came, and I had no idea what to do. My GPA was average, my internships were unimpressive, my network was nonexistent, and my résumé did not exist. I went to college to have a good time. I did just enough to get by and fell into the trap of thinking that because I was passing, I was preparing, and let me tell you, those two are not even close to being the same. You can graduate college without have actually prepared yourself for anything. I loved my time in college, but I would have enjoyed it more if I had focused on becoming the person I am today.

Everything I have spoken about in this book leads up to this moment, the days after your college graduation. Once you cross that stage, have your party, and head home, the real world will be waiting for you. We are almost at the end of our journey, with just one stop left: the real world.

CHAPTER 9:

THE REAL WORLD

When I started outlining this book in the summer of 2018, this chapter was not going to be included. The original idea was to take you through your college graduation and end with a summary. That summary will still be included in Chapter 10. I was hesitant to add this chapter because, unlike high school and college, I, as a person and professional, am still very much in this part of my life. Furthermore, there are several things about going to school that most, if not all, students can find some common ground on. Being an adult in the real world is something that can be incredibly vague and far reaching.

For this chapter, I am going to revert back to what I know and what other college graduates have told me. I want to talk about what to be prepared for once you graduate and enter into the working world. Much like the rest of this book, many the topics I discuss aren't taught in schools. This is not necessarily the schools' fault. It is on you to understand the gravity of the situation. It is on you, the individual, to understand the importance of being prepared for every major step in your life. Therefore, let's walk through some things you will experience in your first few years after college.

I want to mention that there is no way to cover everything about this part of your life in one chapter. Every topic I list here could probably have its own chapter. Also, I am positive that there are additional topics and subtopics that I am missing.

This is just something to help you get started and avoid some of the common pitfalls after graduation.

The truth about corporate America: money is what matters.

The cold, hard truth about corporate America is that every single company exists to make money. Even nonprofits have missions to fund and bills to pay. The companies you will be applying to are designed to make profits. Larger companies have investors and board members who mainly care about the company's "bottom line" or how much money they are making after they pay their expenses. Therefore, if they are going to hire you, that means they are spending money on you, and if they are spending money on you, they want to know how you are going to make them money in return. They want to know what kind of value you are going to bring to the organization. They will care about your output more than anything else. They will not care about your feelings, your student loan debt, or that your parents think you're a good person. If you do not perform at the job you were hired for, they will replace you with someone who will.

Now, I am not saying that every single person in corporate America is a greedy jerk. You will encounter coworkers whom you will enjoy working with and may even become friends with. You will have bosses who will guide you and help you in becoming a better employee and more capable person. What I am saying is that the corporate world is a lot tougher than the classroom. Things move faster, and the expectation is that you applied to the job because you understand all it encompasses and you can keep up and perform.

Don't take the job-application process personally.

When I graduated from college, I applied to hundreds of jobs for 3 years before I landed my first job in my field of study. Part of the reason for that was that I had a weak résumé and no references who would vouch for me. Another reason was that I graduated during a recession, a time where companies were very conservative about whom they were hiring. Part of the reason, though, was merely the application process itself.

Every company has its own process of accepting applications and screening candidates. For example, some can be as simple as filling out a few fields online about yourself and submitting a résumé. Then, you likely have a phone interview with human resources (HR), followed by an in-person interview with the hiring manager before they make the decision. Others can be much more complicated. Many companies are still using older systems in which you not only have to upload a résumé, but then re-enter all that information manually, which can be tedious and time consuming. Larger companies tend to have several rounds of interviews because of the high volume of applicants. You may get a phone call from HR, followed by one or two phone interviews, followed by one, two, or even three in-person interviews before they make their choice.

You could have been the most qualified applicant, but sometimes it is just a numbers game.

It's also important to know that just because you applied to a job does not mean anyone actually saw your résumé. First, it varies who actually sees your résumé initially. It could be someone from HR or recruiting and not the actual hiring manager. This means that someone who does not work in your field at all is determining whether you qualify for the position. This person is only looking for whatever the hiring manager told him or her to look for. You could be removed from the process despite being qualified. Also, you could have been the 21st person to apply to the job, and the original résumé screener decided to stop at the 20th résumé. You could have been the most qualified applicant, but sometimes it is just a numbers game.

Lastly, companies will not openly admit this, but they often post positions before they get actual approval. They also forget to take jobs off the website or job boards after they are filled, meaning that you could be applying to a job that does not actually exist. That does not happen often, but it is essential to know before you get down on yourself. Additionally, they often post publicly because they have to, but have already leaned toward promoting from within. Don't let yourself get discouraged.

Remember that applying for that first job is an uphill battle, and you should try to do anything you can to make the process just a little easier on yourself.

What I am trying to say is don't be too hard on yourself when you are applying for jobs. Just because you did not get an interview does not mean you were not qualified. There are a lot of factors at play, and some of them are just not fair. Be sure to have a solid résumé and cover letter. After you apply, try to find someone at that company who is also on LinkedIn and send them a short note explaining your interest in the position. Remember that applying for that first job is an uphill battle, and you should try to do anything you can to make the process just a little easier on yourself.

You may not like your first job.

You could do everything right throughout high school and college. You could follow all the steps, processes, and advice I have given you. You could build a vast network, have a great résumé, do a ton of research, and apply to and get a job in your field. You could do all this and still not enjoy your first job. The key here is to not panic. Do not think you made a mistake. Entry-level jobs are not the most exciting positions in the company.

When you take an entry-level job, you are basically the lowest person on the totem pole. Oftentimes, the more tedious, boring tasks will fall to you. They may not let someone fresh out of college work on the big, exciting projects right away. This does not mean you did something wrong or have fallen off track. It simply means you need to work hard at those tedious tasks and work your way toward more challenging opportunities. It may be frustrating that after years of researching this field, dreaming of all the exciting projects you thought you'd be working on, that you are currently filling out spreadsheets, taking minutes of the meetings, planning meetings, or doing something that leaves you unfulfilled. This is something that you have to push through.

Most career advisors will tell you that you must stay at your first job for at least 1 year. I don't necessarily disagree with that, but I would like to add a layer to it. Staying in your first career job for a year shows that you can be loyal to a company and shows that you can be employed for an extended length of time. However, I would suggest you conduct the following audit at the 6-month mark.

First-Job Audit

1. Am I learning something new almost every day?
2. Am I spending at least part of my time working on projects related to my studies?
3. Am I moving toward becoming the person I have been building in my head?
4. Is this job what I expected it to be?
   a. If no, why is that?
5. Is the company bringing in new employees or laying off the current ones?
6. Is this a stable company that I can grow with?

You are asking yourself these questions to gain an understanding of how much you are growing with a company.

Again, you should not expect to grow leaps and bounds every day. If you are learning and growing, even at a slow pace, on a daily or weekly basis, then you should want to stay and continue to grow. If you can see yourself moving into a new position, then it is probably worth staying.

However, if you are not growing at all and are never learning new things, that could be a red flag. If the job you are doing is not what you were hired for, that is another red flag. Lastly, if the company never hires new people or replaces those who leave, that could be the sign of financial troubles. If you are seeing all of these red flags and feel that your job or career might be in jeopardy, then you do have the right to look elsewhere.

The last thing I will say about your job is that sometimes, a day is just a day. Meaning: not every single day will be exciting. You will not always have something cool to report on when you get home. No matter what job you have, at any point in your career, you will have regular days. A problem only arises when everyday's like this, and you find yourself no longer learning and growing.

Every Job Has Its Bad Days

There is a saying that you have most likely heard several times in your life (in fact, we discussed it in Chapter 3): "Find a job you love, and you will never work a day in your life." I hate this saying. I hate it so much that every time I hear it, I want to scream. I hate it for two reasons. First, it is flat out not true. Anything worth having in life you have to work for. If you want a six-figure salary, a big house, and a fancy car, you are going to have to work hard for those things. You are going to have to do things not because you want to, but because you have to. The second reason I hate it is because it sets unreal expectations that there is a "perfect job" out there that is always sunshine and rainbows. That job does not exist.

Your job and career are not meant to be a source of constant joy and happiness. You have noticed that I seldom use the word "happiness" throughout this book. Happiness means nothing but positive things. Your job is not going to bring you happiness. You may enjoy working there, and the things you accomplish and the people you help might make you happy, but you will not always feel that way. Even if you climb to the top of the mountain you have created for yourself, and you have become that person you have worked towards, you will still have bad days at work.

Your job may be hard and stressful, but if—at the end of the day, week, month, and year—you can look back and say you made the type of impact you were aiming for, that is what can give you a sense of overall happiness.

You are always going to have days at work that are stressful. You are not always going to wake up with a strong desire to go to work that day. You may come home some days very angry because a project isn't working, a sale fell through, or a coworker messed something up. However, if you take the time to prepare for this part of life, understand what you are passionate about, and pursue a career that lets you be the person you want to be, then you should come home from work most days with a feeling of accomplishment and pride. Your job may be hard and stressful, but if—at the end of the day, week, month, and year—you can look back and say you made the type of impact you were aiming for, that is what can give you a sense of overall happiness.

Finances and Retirement (401k)

When I survey graduates about their regrets and things they were not prepared for, one topic that comes up is finances. Many graduates felt they were not adequately educated on how to save, invest, or budget their money. You will notice that I hardly ever criticize the educational system in this country throughout this book. I genuinely believe that this is a time for you as an individual to take responsibility to learn these lessons on your own. However, when it comes to finances, I will take our educational system to task.

Up until this point, everything you needed was there; you just needed to know where to look. This is different. Your school will not teach you these fundamental skills. This is on you.

We have to find a way to work these topics into the basic math curriculum in high schools. Let me be clear: I do not blame teachers for not teaching this. I blame the government for forcing instructors to teach other types of math that are only used by some people while leaving no time for the topics that will affect almost everyone. Throughout this book, I have positioned school and your education as something to pay attention to and take advantage of. Up until this point, everything you needed was there; you just needed to know where to look. This is different. Your school will not teach you these fundamental skills. This is on you.

Most students are not thinking about life right after graduation because it is 4-8 years away. So, imagine how unlikely it is that you are going to be thinking about retirement, which is over 40 years away. However, this is what came up when I asked former grads what they were most unprepared for when they were starting their careers. Some did not even bother contributing to retirement, or what's called a 401(k), until they were in their late 20s or early 30s. By then, you are behind the curve, playing catch-up to ensure that you have enough money to retire. Taking control of your future does not stop when you graduate college.

Like I have said countless times, you need to listen to those who have come before you. People who were once in your shoes were not prepared and, therefore, made mistakes that affected their quality of life in one way or another.

When you start your first job, HR will most likely present you with your options for contributing to your 401(k). However, if you don't understand the importance of it, you probably will not take it seriously or ask too many questions. Plus, you may not be that inclined to put money away for something that you won't be able to touch for decades, particularly when you have to pay those student loan bills right now and every month. Like I have said countless times, you need to listen to those who have come before you. People who were once in your shoes were not prepared and, therefore, made mistakes that affected their quality of life in one way or another.

Make sure you fully understand your 401(k), retirement plan, and pension, if your job offers you one. If you don't quite grasp what HR is explaining to you, then ask questions. If you still don't understand, talk to your parents or other coworkers. Take control of the situation. Consult with a financial advisor about what the best plan is for you. Talk with that person about investing. You do not have to know everything about the stock market, but develop a method where your money starts to work for you. Again, you won't see the benefits of this overnight, but you can move through your life knowing that you will be okay when retirement comes. If not, you are going to spend a lot of time being stressed, worrying whether you are saving enough to have enough money to retire.

Lastly, learn how to create a budget. Budgeting is something a lot of people struggle with, me included. Therefore, it would be irresponsible for me to try and create some master plan for you to follow. Budgeting is unique to the individual: how much you make; how much your spouse, if you have one, makes; and how much you can afford to save after all your expenses. Here are two pieces of advice. First, open up a savings account before you start work. When you fill out the paperwork for your direct deposit for your first job, split up which accounts your money goes into. For example, for several years, the first $200 of my paycheck went into my savings account. That comes out to $400 a month, and $4,800 for the year. It's essential to have a savings account like this because random expenses will pop up in your life. Your car will break down, you will need to buy new clothes for work, your friends start to get married and you will be in the wedding party, and a host of other things that will cost more money than you currently have in your bank account. If you have a savings account to draw from, you will not have to use your credit cards.

Speaking of credit cards, let's talk about them, because it appears this is another topic that people were not educated on before they entered the real world. A credit card can be a very dangerous thing. You can use it to pay for something when you do not have the money in your checking account. At first, it seems like a fantastic thing. It feels like free money. The issue is, though, if you don't have the money to pay for it now, how do you expect to have the money down the line, when your expenses and paycheck are basically the same? Furthermore, every purchase you make has interest attached to it, just like your student loans. For example, if you buy something for $100 and your interest rate is 10%, then you are going to owe $110 if you do not pay it off right away. You'll end up paying even more for something you couldn't afford in the first place.

My second and last piece of advice on this is to find yourself an expert on these topics and consult with that person. There are a ton of books and videos on the subject, and financial professionals who are there to help you, but just like your teachers, you have to take advantage of the opportunities they are giving you. Whether it's someone your parents know or someone you find on your own, find yourself a trustworthy financial advisor who can help you understand your 401(k), all the taxes you have to pay, how to budget your money, and what to invest in throughout your career. This will help you avoid costly mistakes, unnecessary stress, and give you the financial freedom to live life on your own terms.

Professionalism in the Workplace

After four internships, you should have a decent idea of how to behave in the workplace. However, it's important to understand how complex an office and a company can be. Plus, in your first full-time role, you will be working with more people, which means dealing with different personalities. You will also be taking on more tasks and more responsibility.

Following are some basic tips to maintain a professional reputation in the workplace.

Show Up to Work on Time

This may seem like an obvious one in theory, but after talking to people who have managed college graduates, it is not in practice. You may end up working in an office in which not everyone shows up at the same time. You may be getting in on time, but the person next to you comes in 10–30 minutes later. This does not mean you should start doing the same.

First, you don't know whether that person has a special arrangement worked out with the boss, or whether his or her position requires working later hours. Second, employees who have been with the company for longer than you may have earned this right, whereas you have not. Third, this person could be plain lazy, and why would want to copy the habits of a lazy person? The last thing you want is to build a reputation as someone who is lazy, or worse, entitled to perks that he or she has not yet earned.

Dress to Impress

You may hear the saying "Dress for the job you want, not that job you have." Well, if you dress like a CEO in a suit when the rest of the office is casual, you will look like an idiot. Again, you don't need to have the reputation of someone who thinks he's better than everyone else. That being said, ask what the dress code is before you start. Be sure to wear nice, ironed out clothes and professional, clean shoes. Show that you are serious about the way you present yourself. Again, you may see people in your office who dress one level above what you wear to bed. Let them make their own mistakes. Stay focused on presenting the image of a hardworking professional on the outside, because you know you are becoming one on the inside.

Follow Up/Respond to E-mails

Learning how to follow up on an e-mail that has not been responded to is tough. It's even tougher when you are asking for an answer or deliverable from a more senior coworker who has missed her deadline. First, understand that an e-mail is not a text to a friend. Second, always know that the person you are emailing is just as busy, if not busier than, you. Give her the benefit of the doubt that she simply missed your previous e-mail, or something popped up that preventing her from sending you what was owed. Lastly, always be polite and do not take it personally. Regardless of how many times you have had to follow up on something, understand that she is not unresponsive to spite you. Always be appreciative of this person's time, even if you do not feel like he or she has been respectful of yours.

Watch Your Mouth

This is a big one. You are at work, not at the bar, or in your friend's basement. Your sense of humor may kill with your friends but may offend someone whose background you know nothing about. Remember when we spoke about meeting new people at college? This is the same idea. When in doubt, keep your mouth shut. Furthermore, when you are one of the newest employees in the office, you will have to keep mum on topics that you want to speak out on. If someone asks for your opinion, provide a respectful response that offers a solution. Do not just pile on to a problem that has already been presented. It's okay to joke around with coworkers whom you are comfortable with, but think before you speak. If you think it's not appropriate for work, just let it go.

Aim for a Work–Life Balance

As we talked about way back in Chapter 1, your full-time job will take up a lot of your time. When you add up your work hours, commuting, sleep, and everything else, almost two-thirds of your week is booked up. Therefore, the free time that you do have is vital to your mental health and general well-being. No matter how much joy and satisfaction you get out of your job, it is still work. It is always something that commands energy and will, at times, generate stress. It's important also to make time in your life for the things that bring you a different type of joy and happiness. It's important to make time for family, friends, and the things and activities that bring you joy.

When you're in school, the class you are in ends at a particular time. The homework you have has a definite end point, and when your studying, you know you're done when you have covered all the topics. Work is different; the work never actually ends. There is always one more e-mail to send, one more task to complete, or a new project you could get a jumpstart on. There is always going to be someone in the office who is still working when you are ready to leave. Do not think you need to work 12-hour days every day to prove yourself. It is okay to go home when the day is done to recharge your mind and body. Yes, on some days, you will have to stay late. But most days, the work can wait until the next day. It's important to go home, spend time with your family, and let yourself relax. Your career is a marathon, even when some days feel like an all-out sprint.

This also goes for vacation days, or personal time off (PTO), as some companies refer to it. You will always have that coworker who brags about how he never takes any time off. Good for him. I am a HUGE believer in using your vacation days throughout the year. It's important to understand that life is more than just the job you are working. It's also important to realize that no matter how busy you are, your department and company will function without you for a few days.

Be sure to put in your request for your anticipated days off as soon as you know you want to take them. Also, gain an understanding of when the busy times for your company are. For example, if your company sells a lot of product in the spring, perhaps try not to use any time off until the summer. If your company/department is "dead" around the holidays, then there is no reason not to put in for that time. Also be sure that when you do take off, someone is prepared to cover your work, if needed. This way you have ensured that everything keeps moving and you can enjoy your time off with a lot less stress.

Outside-the-Box Careers

This is something that is close to my heart. It is especially relevant to me and the journey I am on. As we've gone over before, one of the main reasons the majority of adults dislike their jobs is because they were not prepared for them. However, there is another reason that certain people dislike what they do for a living and the life they are currently in. This happens when people who were destined for something unique end up doing something routine or ordinary.

At some point in your life, whether it be high school, college, or the real world, you may decide you want something different out of life. You may want to pursue a career that is considered unusual, risky, or outside the box.

What I mean by this is that we live in a society that encourages everyone to take the same career path. From a young age, you are encouraged to go to school, get good grades, and get a good, safe job. Your parents and teachers will often try to deter you from any type of career that is deemed unsafe or unlikely to work out. The reason is that they want to protect you. The number one priority for your parents is to keep you safe. They do not want to see you fail or get hurt, so if they think that might happen, it is their natural inclination to steer you to safety. Therefore, you are encouraged to take a safe, routine job, at a good company with good benefits. For some, this is a perfect route to take. If the person you have decided to come falls in line with this way of thinking, there is entirely nothing wrong with that.

At some point in your life, whether it be high school, college, or the real world, you may decide you want something different out of life. You may want to pursue a career that is considered unusual, risky, or outside the box. Whether it be acting, writing, signing, sports broadcasting, public speaking, or one of the many other unique professions that are out there, you may decide that you want to do something different. You may feel this way for many reasons. After sitting in a cubicle for a few years, you may decide that it is not for you. If you want to be the type of person who entertains others, then there might not be able to find an office job that aligns with your passion. Whatever the case, if you feel that you want to pursue a different kind of career, then you have to do it.

This is precisely what happened to me. If I had followed my own advice, I would have discovered two things: (1) I will not enjoy sitting at a desk for 8 hours a day, and (2) I want to become the type of person who helps AND entertains people on a daily basis. I would have majored in journalism, not public relations, and I would most likely have a job that lets be me more of myself.

When you have the audacity to chase your dreams, you remind others that they never had the courage to pursue their dreams.

If you decide to take the leap and pursue something different, be prepared for resistance. Your family members will likely question how you are going to make money doing that and how are you going to support yourself. They'll point out everything that could go wrong. You might also have friends who will point out that it probably won't work and that you don't understand what you're doing. Here is the thing to remember: when you have the audacity to chase your dreams, you remind others that they never had the courage to pursue their *own* dreams. Thus, they get angry and try to stop you. You need to ignore those people and surround yourself with people who support your dreams. Listen to the family members who either chased their dreams or at least understand why you are chasing yours. Find the friends who "get it" and honestly want you to succeed. I am lucky enough to have almost nothing but positive support from my family and friends. However, based on the conversations I have had with others, this is not always the case. Remember, there is nothing wrong with working in an office from 9 to 5. There is also nothing wrong with wanting something different for yourself.

Being an Adult

At the beginning of this book, we talked about the real world being made up of two things: working full time and being an adult. We've covered a lot of aspects of planning, working, and building your career. We also talked about becoming an adult by making that list of things our parents do for us and then starting to take over items and do them for ourselves. Being an adult means taking full responsibility for every aspect of your life. It means knowing that the world you are about to enter is expecting you to act and react in a certain way.

You are responsible for everyday tasks such as getting yourself up for work, cooking your meals, shopping for your food, and making your own doctors' appointments. You are responsible for ensuring that you are prepared for work, eating right, and living a healthy lifestyle. When you enter the workplace, your coworkers are going to treat you the way they are treated. They are going to expect that you "grew up" in college and are prepared for the job you are hired for. If someone is rude to you, you cannot call your mom and complain. If your boss yells at you, you cannot just storm into HR or quit your job. These are situations you will face, and because you are an adult, you will have to come up with solutions on your own.

Being an adult means doing the not-so-fun stuff on a regular basis. It means understanding finances, paying your bills, understanding and paying your taxes, and a host of other less-than-exciting things. I don't say all this to depress you; I say it to prepare you. If you understand what is going to be expected ahead of time, you can spend your time leading up to and preparing for it. You can ask the questions, do the research, and practice the habits you need to make adulthood easier on yourself.

As I said at the beginning of this chapter, the real world is so much more than just these few pages. If you have enjoyed our conversation, I invite you to look out for my next book in this series AND for my online course. Both projects will be designed to dive deeply into the various aspects of the real world and how you can continue to become the person you want to be and to build a life you want to live.

We are just about at the end of our conversation. One last chapter to go.

Chapter 10:
This Is Where I Leave You

We have reached the final chapter and the close of what has hopefully been a beneficial conversation for you. As I said, it is my desire to create a book that any student can pick up, at any point in their journey, and use the advice, processes, and checklists provided to help build a life that they will enjoy living for decades to come. It is my hope that what I offered in this book has given you the confidence you need to tackle the next steps in your life. I hope that you are now feeling more comfortable with the choices you need to make to take control of your education, future, and life.

However, it is possible that you have reached the end of this book feeling incomplete. It is entirely possible that you feel I left out specific instructions on how to accomplish the various steps laid out in this book. You may have been expecting this to be a strictly how-to book that covers every step of everything you need to do. As you can tell, this is not that book, and I left a lot of that out on purpose.

The real world is packed with situations that you need to navigate by yourself, and the whole point of this book is to prepare you for those scenarios.

I left out specific instructions because it is time for you to take control of your choices. It's time to take ownership of and responsibility for your future. If I gave you step-by-step instructions to follow, how would you ever learn to do these things on your own? The real world is packed with situations that you need to navigate by yourself, and the whole point of this book is to prepare you for those scenarios. If I told you everything you need to do to apply to college, then I would have done you a grave disservice. First, the college selection process is unique to you as a person. Any one-size-fits-all approach would be incomplete and borderline useless.

Second, if I removed the effort from the process, then you wouldn't be as invested in it. If I told you what to do and when to do it, you would merely be going through the motions and never getting mentally prepared for the situation and environment you are striving for. When you put time and energy into something, you are mentally invested in the outcome and are much more likely to care about what happens next.

The same type of logic goes for reaching out to and networking with college alumni and working professionals. It is my job to tell you why you should be reaching out and what the topic of conversation should be. With that being said, if I wrote the e-mails for you, you would never learn how to network on your own. Not to mention, when reaching out to someone and asking for advice, you want to make it as personal as possible.

Lastly, there are certain topics that I am simply not an expert on. I never went for my master's, nor have I been to community college. I don't have the best advice for SAT prep and writing your college essay. I am also not a financial expert or résumé professional. The point of all this was to persuade you to care so much about your future that you seek out the information you need on all these topics and to find that information from real experts who are ready to give it to you.

What I am trying to say is this: if you feel like I left out how to actually do something, there was a reason for it. We all go through the same educational system, more or less, and we all end up as adults in the real world (some more adult than others). However, that is where the similarities tend to end. Everyone needs to lead their own journey and figure out these next steps on their own. The problem we have now is that everyone is looking for a quick fix, or worse, someone to copy so they can get it done faster and avoid the stress of difficult situations. Hopefully, you understand what the end result needs to be and why it's so important to achieve it.

Even though we did not go into specifics, we did cover a lot of ground. The following is a recap of some of the main points I am trying to make. These are the most important takeaways and the things I believe in the most. It's also a section that you can refer back to over the years when you feel you have lost your way, or your vision of the future becomes blurry.

Remember the Type of Person You Envision

By now, you may be sick of hearing me talk about the type of person you want to become. I have hit it home in nearly every chapter. I did that for a reason. This is the backbone of every single thing you will do from here on out. You may change schools, majors, jobs, or careers over the years, but you will never change what type of person you want to become. It may evolve and expand, but the core of who you want to be as a person—and the legacy you want to leave behind—will remain the same.

Remember this when things get tough. Keep this person in mind when obstacles such as getting rejected from a college, failing a test, or not getting that job pop up along the way. This is what keeps me going on my journey as a youth motivational speaker and book author. Any time I get turned down for a speaking engagement or hit writer's block when writing my blog, I remember that I want to become the type of person who helps students build better futures. Your journey will be tough, and the real world will be even tougher. If you keep that person and the life you want to build in mind, you can get through anything and keep pushing toward that end goal.

Understand the Importance of Education

Before you take another step, you need to change your attitude toward education. Most students don't like school. Almost all of the college graduates I surveyed said they did not care for school. No matter what, you are going to take classes you don't care for. You will take courses that you find dull. Never forget where you are going and the importance the education you are receiving to get there.

If you are lucky enough to sit a classroom and expand your knowledge, then you are better off than many others. There are thousands of former students who, for one reason or another, had to cut their education short, or were never opened up to the ideas and information that you have the chance to learn. Attending class, doing homework, and studying for tests should no longer be treated as chores that you are forced to do.

They should be approached as things you want to do, as well as possible. Remember, you may not like certain classes, but you should love the idea of living a life of joy and satisfaction.

Take Advantage of Your Opportunities

This is another point I have hit on consistently. High school, college, and everything in between are going to present you with a series of opportunities that have the ability to give you the knowledge, skills, and experience needed to not only be prepared for the real world but also to thrive in it once you get there. Just like you are going to change your approach to education, you are going to change your approach to how you view everyday life.

You should wake up every day thinking about how to find ways to become a better student, a smarter person, and the person you have been building in your head. Some days you will find massive opportunities like an internship to apply to or an event to attend. Most days the opportunities will be harder to see, but just as valuable. It can be as simple as staying after class to ask questions about your upcoming test. You may need to do something proactive such as message a working professional on LinkedIn or stop by your career center to review your résumé. The key is to train your brain to look for opportunities in all situations. Make identifying ways to better yourself a habit.

Learn About Your Future Career

All the way back in Chapter 1, I mentioned why I started this entire journey. Do you remember what it was? It was because I have spent years working with people who disliked their jobs and the type of lives they are living. We have covered the various reasons as to why this is, but most of those reasons come back to not understanding the career they were signing up for. Your high school and college years are a time to understand exactly what you are working toward.

If you want to live a life on your own terms, you need to have a complete understanding of how your chosen career is going to affect and fit into that life.

If you think you know what job or career you want to pursue, always be sure to learn as much about that profession as possible. You should know what the starting and average salaries are, how easy or difficult it is to get a job in that field, how much education you will need (and need to pay for), and what a typical schedule is like. You may think you want a certain career until you find out how much it pays or how much more schooling you'd need. If, in your self-discovery, you find that job security and spending time with family is important to you, that may disqualify some jobs that sound great but require long and constantly changing hours.

Be sure to paint a full picture for yourself. Most people don't do that, and they are shocked to find out that what they thought was their dream job wasn't dreamy at all. Most of these people never even bothered to pick a dream job. Instead, they chose something they thought they might like and then ended up spending the majority of the week doing something they don't enjoy at all. If you want to live a life on your own terms, you need to have a complete understanding of how your chosen career is going to affect and fit into that life.

Build a Life You Want to Live

This one is pretty similar to the previous point, but it covers a lot more ground. As we have spoken about, your career is going to take up a significant amount of time and impact your life in many ways. The reason I stress the importance of doing research, conducting internal audits, and being prepared is so that you end up living a life that you are happy to live. Keep this in mind when making various choices along the way.

There is no reason to enter into a career and then be completely caught off guard regarding what it entails and what is expected of you.

For example, if you want to live a life that allows you to travel, that takes money. So, you may not want to take out a large student loan just to go to that big, fancy school. You may want to find a smaller school, perhaps less known but just as a credible, and save that fancy-school money for yourself. When figuring out who you are and what you want in life, you may discover that you want to have a career that lets you make your own schedule or one that provides different, exciting things to do every day. If that's the life you want to live, then you need to research possible professions to see whether this fits into that type of life.

Lastly, you may not want to be the type of person who has to work nights, weekends, and holidays. If being home at those times is important to you, then you need to be sure you are pursuing a profession that will let you do that. There is no reason to enter into a career and then be completely caught off guard regarding what it entails and what is expected of you.

Remember Why You Started

There are going to be a lot of times along the way where you will get tired of being the type of person who tries their hardest, does the research, puts in the work, and prioritizes opportunities over shortcuts. When you are applying to colleges, there are going to be weekends during which you would rather hang out with your friends than visit schools or research them online. When you get to college, there will always be something funner than going to class, meeting with an advisor, attending an event, or going to the library. Once you enter the real world, it will be easy to take the first job you find or stay in a position that allows you to do just enough to get by. When you get tired or become tempted to stop trying so hard, remember why you started. Remember why you chose to prepare for your future ahead of time rather than figure it out later.

Those people are now living lives they never intended on living. They wake up every day and go to jobs they don't like and come home feeling uninspired and unfulfilled.

Keep in mind all the people who have come before you who did not do what you are doing—the thousands of people who didn't take school seriously, didn't plan for their futures, and didn't do what needed to be done. Those people are now living lives they never intended on living. They wake up every day and go to jobs they don't like and come home feeling uninspired and unfulfilled. At the beginning of this book, I spoke about the hours of your week and how your job takes up two-thirds of your time. That is a lot of time to be unhappy simply because you did not care enough to prepare for your future. Bear in mind what working full time is actually like and all the adult responsibilities that are coming your way.

The two main things that should keep you motivated are the life you want to live when you enter the real world and the life you absolutely *do not* want to get stuck living when you enter the real world. This entire book is about taking control of your life and your future. The idea of living life on your own terms should be reason enough to stay on this journey and work as hard and as long as it takes.

The key is not to attempt to build a life that is full of nothing but happiness. The key is to build a life that has purpose—a purpose that results in self-satisfaction and a positive impact on the community and people around you, a purpose that helps people and makes this world a better place.

Life is hard. Being an adult is difficult. The real world is complicated and unfair. There is nothing you can do in high school or college that will fix those facts. There is nothing I could say to help you avoid these hard truths. Begin to understand that no matter what you do, how hard your work, or what career you pursue, you will always have difficult times. You will always have bad days. You will at times feel stress. The key is not to attempt to build a life that is full of nothing but happiness. The key is to build a life that has purpose—a purpose that results in self-satisfaction and a positive impact on the community and people around you, a purpose that helps people and makes this world a better place. If you can create a life that does these things, it will help carry you through the dark times. The bad days won't seem as bad, and the stressful situations won't last as long. It won't be as bad because you will know you are living a life of purpose. You are living a life that you can be proud of. You are living life on your own terms.

No matter where you are in your educational journey, it is never too late to start determining what type of person you want to become. It is never too late to decide that you are going to take control of your future and build your own life. I hope that you are inspired to begin that journey, no matter where you are.

If you are a parent and/or a college graduate reading this book, I hope that you understand and agree with my message. I hope that you share this book with any student in your life. Take these lessons, ideas, and themes and encourage students to apply them to their day-to-day life. We need to prepare younger generations for the real world. We need to support these young, energetic, idealistic students to follow their dreams, to inspire them to make a difference in this world. We need to show them that the real world is not something you are doomed to trudge through, but rather an opportunity to create a life they will be excited to live.

To the student reading this book, I believe in you. I believe in the power of education and I believe in the power of taking advantage of your opportunities. I also believe that this world desperately needs more people doing what they are passionate about. Our future generations must pursue careers that align with their passions. The positive effects that will result from this type of shift in thinking will be massive. It all starts with you.

I wish you nothing but the best from here on out. I encourage you to share this book with your friends and inspire them to join you. I also encourage you to re-read this book along your journey to stay energized and motivated.

Best of luck to you. I'm rooting for you. Thanks for talking. Goodbye.

-Kyle

TO MY EARLY SUPPORTERS

A special THANK YOU to everyone who pre-ordered my book when it was nothing but an idea and a dream. Your support and belief in me helped make this a reality. I will always appreciate and cherish the support you gave and continue to give.

Kayla Grappone
The Grappone Family
The McKavanagh Family
Maureen McCabe-Kours
The Alfano Family
The Sengelaub Family
The DellAnno Family
The Schwetz Family
Ian and Rachel Jackson
Jeff Lucisano
Laura Kaufherr
Dan and Kaitlyn O'Connor
Alyssa Marinaro
Angelina Minutolo
Anthony Gough
Barbara DiGangi
The Cavacchioli Family
Greg Chaves

Jack Collins
Jack Nightingale
Jillian Paff
Sally Christophedes
Joey Fantozzi
Chris and Kate Boydston
Kim Rail
Lee and Linda Clapp
Mike Poast
The Bistany Family
Paul and Amy Zegers
Peter King
Peter McCabe
Sean Reynolds
Teia Gillard
The McGrath Family
The Gallway Family
William Murphy

Richard and Nancy Cariello
Matthew D'Angelico and Julie Tuzzolino
Alan Damiani and Christine Foltz
Diana Tarello and Jimmy Ketterer
James Lennon and Charlotte Barrett
George and Denise Galiatsatos
Jessie Resnick and Anthony Colasacco
Robert and Megan Kellert
Shawn and Nicole Aupperlee

ABOUT ATMOSPHERE PRESS

Atmosphere Press is an independent, full-service publisher for books in genres ranging from nonfiction to fiction to poetry, with a special emphasis on being an author-friendly approach to the challenges of getting a book into the world. Learn more about what we do at atmospherepress.com.

We encourage you to check out some of Atmosphere's latest releases, which are available at Amazon.com and via order from your local bookstore:

The George Stories, a novel by Christopher Gould
No Home Like a Raft, poetry by Martin Jon Porter
Mere Being, poetry by Barry D. Amis
The Traveler, a young adult novel by Jennifer Deaver
Channel: How to be a Clear Channel for Inspiration by Listening, Enjoying, and Trusting Your Intuition, nonfiction by Jessica Ang
Mandated Happiness, a novel by Clayton Tucker
The Third Door, a novel by Jim Williams
Love Your Vibe: Using the Power of Sound to Take Command of Your Life, nonfiction by Matt Omo
The Yoga of Strength, a novel by Andrew Marc Rowe
They are Almost Invisible, poetry by Elizabeth Carmer
Let the Little Birds Sing, a novel by Sandra Fox Murphy
Carpenters and Catapults: A Girls Can Do Anything Book, children's fiction by Carmen Petro
Spots Before Stripes, a novel by Jonathan Kumar
Auroras over Acadia, poetry by Paul Liebow
Gone Fishing: A Girls Can Do Anything Book, children's fiction by Carmen Petro

Owlfred the Owl, a picture book by Caleb Foster
Transcendence, poetry and images by Vincent Bahar Towliat
Leaving the Ladder: An Ex-Corporate Girl's Guide from the Rat Race to Fulfilment, nonfiction by Lynda Bayada
Adrift, poems by Kristy Peloquin
Letting Nicki Go: A Mother's Journey through Her Daughter's Cancer, nonfiction by Bunny Leach
Time Do Not Stop, poems by William Guest
Dear Old Dogs, a novella by Gwen Head
Bello the Cello, a picture book by Dennis Mathew
How Not to Sell: A Sales Survival Guide, nonfiction by Rashad Daoudi
Ghost Sentence, poems by Mary Flanagan
That Scarlett Bacon, a picture book by Mark Johnson
Such a Nice Girl, a novel by Carol St. John
Makani and the Tiki Mikis, a picture book by Kosta Gregory
What Outlives Us, poems by Larry Levy
Winter Park, a novel by Graham Guest
That Beautiful Season, a novel by Sandra Fox Murphy
What I Cannot Abandon, poems by William Guest
All the Dead Are Holy, poems by Larry Levy
Rescripting the Workplace: Producing Miracles with Bosses, Coworkers, and Bad Days, nonfiction by Pam Boyd
Surviving Mother, a novella by Gwen Head
Who Are We: Man and Cosmology, poetry by William Guest

ABOUT KYLE GRAPPONE

Kyle Grappone is a youth motivational speaker, book author, and student coach. His goal is to inspire students to think differently about their education and future. He believes in the importance of getting today's students prepared to enter the real world that awaits them. He does this by asking students "What type of person do you want to become?" He believes by asking this question, students can begin to discover their passions and use that discovery to pursue a career that will deliver purpose and satisfaction.

Kyle started this journey after nearly 10 years working in the real world. A few years after college, he began to notice that many of the people who he worked with seemed to dislike their jobs and were unhappy with the type of person they had become. When he began to research this by surveying his coworkers and college graduates, he began to discover that the main reason for this was because people were not prepared for the next steps in life. They did not understand what being an adult and working full time actually meant.

He believes that many former students, himself included, developed an "I'll figure it out later" type of attitude. Then, later finally came and they were thrown into a world they knew nothing about, forced to take a job they did not want, and ended up living a life they never intended on living.

This is what fuels Kyle's passion. He works every day to inspire students to prepare for the real world by discovering their passions and taking control of their futures. His dream is to see generations of students who are working in careers aligned with the type of person they want to become and the type of impact they wish to have on the world.

If you would like to learn more about Kyle, his speaking engagements, or his coaching services, please e-mail him at Kyle@KyleGrappone.com.

CPSIA information can be obtained
at www.ICGtesting.com
Printed in the USA
LVHW032226020919
629674LV00006B/736/P